mikey and me

life with my exceptional sister

Teresa Sullivan

SHE WRITES PRESS

Published 2017
Printed in the United States of America
Print ISBN: 978-1-63152-270-3
E-ISBN: 978-1-63152-271-0
Library of Congress Control Number: 2017940090

For information, address:
She Writes Press
1563 Solano Ave #546
Berkeley, CA 94707

Cover design © Julie Metz, Ltd./metzdesign.com
Interior design by Tabitha Lahr

She Writes Press is a division of SparkPoint Studio, LLC.

Names and identifying characteristics have been changed to
protect the privacy of certain individuals.

For Mikey
and
for our parents

contents

PART THREE—INTERLUDE

PART FOUR—PASSAGES

part one

Bits of Beets and Tadpoles

beets

The house I grew up in looked like any other on the block. It was a rose-colored, stucco, three-bedroom ranch-style house on an extra-large lot in a middle-class neighborhood in Santa Monica, California, about three miles inland from the Pacific Ocean. There were white shutters on the windows, a shady covered front porch, and a huge living room picture window that Mom decorated with snow-in-a-can "Happy Holidays" at Christmas. A white wrought-iron gate protected the entrance to our huge backyard, which was enclosed by a cinderblock wall. A mass of untended pink geraniums flourished all along the other side of the house. The driveway was large enough to park our tan-and-white Ford station wagon and an old blue Lincoln.

Inside, there was food on the walls, particularly in the dining room. Canned shoestring beets stuck stubbornly to the pink and gray wallpaper. Some of the stains had been there for years. Black and virtually impossible to remove once dry, they blended well with the thin black lines in the pattern.

Dad had painted the rest of the walls in the house a high-gloss tan. Naugahyde had replaced fabric furniture. My grandmother bought us brown linoleum that looked like pebbles, and it covered the floors throughout the house. Everything could be easily swept and wiped clean. The wallpaper in the dining room was all that remained from the days before food was airborne, and it no longer went with anything. Maybe it reminded Mom of when she first decorated her new home, happy and optimistic about raising her girls here.

Even when my sister Mikey was eight years old—one year older than I was—she was like a two-year-old. She didn't speak. She was brain damaged. That was the diagnosis given by a neurologist. She was blind, too.

Flying beets were not the only food adorning our walls, but they were the most plentiful. A brief foray into the kitchen refrigerator yielded a handful of the squishy red vegetable that Mikey had flung during a gleeful spin around the room. With a broad grin on her face and her arms swinging, she squeezed the beets between her fingers and they landed everywhere. Then, in a paradox of manners, she wiped her hand clean on her hair. Sometimes she flung food in a fit of frustration, moments before she clenched her forearm in her teeth, tearing at the flesh.

We never moved the furniture—not even a little bit. Everything was pushed up against the walls. There were no rugs or coffee tables, nothing Mikey could bump into or trip over. Keeping the rooms safe and predictable allowed her to move easily around the house. We were all responsible for keeping doors wide open; a partially open door meant Mikey could smash right into it, face first.

The dining room contained only two pieces of furniture. One, a large, overstuffed, armless black Naugahyde chair, Mikey's chair, was pushed into a corner. She sat in her chair for hours, squeezing Play-Doh between her fingers or bending the lid of a tin can back and forth until a piece broke off and fell to the floor. Without pausing, she continued to bend, working on a new piece. There were small cuts on most of her fingers. She rocked and bent for hours. We didn't take her treasures from her. She enjoyed rifling through the kitchen trashcan to find them and bending seemed to make her happy, to calm her.

In another corner of the dining room stood an antique china cabinet, a family heirloom. It was a golden-oak color with carved lion's feet and a curved glass door. My grandmother had purchased it when she got engaged. It was an expensive indulgence and the nicest thing she ever owned.

After her parents died, Mom brought the cabinet to California from Illinois, had it refinished, and slowly filled it with pieces of pottery and china, including a pair of Santa Claus cups. Mom filled one of them half-full of milk every Christmas Eve, and we set it out, along with a plate of cookies, for Santa. I knew he had come, not only because there were presents, but also because on Christmas morning the cup was empty and Santa had eaten all but half of one cookie. A beautiful china pitcher, painted with purple grapes and green vines, sat on the middle shelf, surrounded by six cups—each painted with a different fruit. My grandmother could never have afforded such fine, hand-painted china and neither could we. I'll bet Mom came across them at one of the auctions she loved. Sometimes she found bargains that she sold for more than they cost, supplementing our income.

It is a mystery to me how the china cabinet remained intact through the years or why it resided in Mikey's favorite room. She could have easily destroyed it during a rampage of biting and flailing. Perhaps it was a defiant line in the sand of adjustments that had to be made to accommodate her.

Mom told me years later that when we first moved into our house in 1955, when Mikey and I were still babies, she visualized our large eat-in kitchen as a center of activity. We would gather every night to share a hearty meal and the events of our day. There would be no distractions, like newspapers, because we would listen to each other. And we would be expected to be on time, and would be, because we'd want to be close with our family. Instead, meals came to represent everything that was different about our home and were a reminder of everything that would never be.

One dinner, when I was seven, stands out. I set the kitchen

table with mismatched Melmac dishes and plastic glasses—nothing breakable. I relished my time alone with Mom, working together to get dinner ready. I told her about my day at school, and she asked occasional questions or offered a bit of praise as she bustled about tasting this and that, making final seasoning adjustments. The scent of cooking onions filled the room when Mom opened the oven door. Pot roast nights were Dad's favorite.

When Dad came home from work and strode into the kitchen that night, he kissed me on top of the head and asked, "How's the terrier today?" Terrier was his nickname for Terry, as I was called back then. I only had a few minutes to talk before Mikey came in, so I spoke in a rush.

Mom and Dad exchanged a few words about how Mikey was doing. They never touched. When he took his seat, Dad opened the evening paper for a brief glance at the news before dinner.

With her Camel dangling from the corner of her mouth, Mom carried our meal to the kitchen table: salad with Thousand Island dressing, pot roast, bread, and oleo. I called out, "Mikey, dinner's ready. Come to the kitchen." She found her seat nearest the kitchen door and sat quietly in the orange plastic chair with her knees pulled up against her chest. Mikey was slender, with fine features, more delicate than mine, and pale translucent skin. Her chin-length brown hair was messy. She was pretty, except for her eyes. They were sunken with no color, only darkness and patches of white.

With Mikey seated, it was time to be quiet. We didn't speak much at dinnertime. It was usually best to keep sensory stimulation to a minimum. Sometimes conversation, a chair dragged across the floor, or the refrigerator door closing overwhelmed Mikey, and she couldn't sit still, couldn't eat, or started biting herself. Some nights we fed her later, after our dinner.

I helped by preparing Mikey's plate with small pieces of cut-up meat, wax beans, and strawberries. Finger foods—nothing too mushy.

It was evident, knowing and observing her, that Mikey's

senses of taste, touch, scent, and sound were heightened. She stilled when she heard the dish set down on the table in front of her. I told her what was on her plate, and she felt for a morsel then picked it up with slender fingers, her pinky daintily extended. She smelled and tasted tentatively. A strawberry. A slight smile crossed her face, as though she was saying "mmmm" while the complex flavors washed over her taste buds.

If she didn't want something, she held it out for someone to take, as if saying, "No, thank you. You can have this." Some food inevitably landed on the floor.

That night, she sat quietly rocking and ate most of her food, then popped up and left the kitchen.

A moment later, the kitchen light went out. Dad called out, "Mikey!" We heard a giggle from the next room, and the light came back on. After we had resumed our dinner, the light went out again. "Mikey!" Mom and I both chimed. She reached around the kitchen door to flip up the light switch, giddy with pleasure. She couldn't see the light, didn't know what light was, but it was great fun. The game went on a few more times, all of us enjoying the play.

After Mikey left, my parents and I could talk. That night, the mood was light as we laughed about Mikey's discovery. We were all delighted by her happiness.

Sometimes, on warm evenings, the neighbor's chubby black dachshund, Jasper, would pad into the kitchen through the open back door. With his nose to the ground, he'd purposefully head straight for Mikey's empty chair. On the floor underneath, he'd find his snack. I always enjoyed his visits, although he was much more interested in the scraps of food than he was in me.

marcile & jim

Mom had a life before she had Mikey and me. I knew because she kept it in the big bottom drawer in the hall, the deepest drawer, underneath the built-in cupboard where we kept sheets and towels. When I was a little girl, I'd plop on the floor, when it was still covered in nubby, gray carpet, and wiggle the sticky wood drawer open to reveal a treasure box of photographs. There were so many that I had to push them down to get the drawer closed again. Mom often sat with me, and as I picked one at a time, told me the stories behind them.

There were pictures of Mikey and me seated in a double stroller. Mikey was clapping her hands, playing patty-cake. I was chubby. That photo was taken during happier times, hopeful times when it seemed like blindness was Mikey's only problem. Mom told me that, when they took us out for a walk, Dad used to walk backward facing Mikey and me in the stroller so that he could look at us. And he beamed when strangers exclaimed how cute we were.

I found yellowed, cardboard photos of severe-looking women with their hair pulled back, dressed in black up to their chins. These were Mom's grandmothers and great-aunts. They

were German Lutheran—solemn farmers' wives—and taught her that it was downright selfish to seek happiness.

In my favorite picture, Mom, her name is Marcile, was about five years old and a shoeless ragamuffin. She was sitting bareback with her six-year-old brother Don on Old Babe, a huge white horse. They rode Babe to the one-room school in their small town of Cullom, Illinois. Mom told me stories about growing up on a farm. They had an outhouse and used pages from the three-inch-thick Sears and Roebuck catalog for toilet paper. I learned about the hobos who came looking for work and food during the Depression, about having to give away egg-sucking dogs if they couldn't keep them out of the chicken coop.

In another picture, Mom's parents, Dora and Earl, posed in front of a barn, a small tractor nearby. Mom described her mother as a strong woman with progressive ideas about farming. Her dad had a short fuse and might have kicked a kid in the rear for a smart-alecky comment. Her big brother, Don, was strong. When they were young, she had to learn to hold her own with him. He grew up to be a hard-working farmer and a heavy drinker. Phyllis, the baby of the family, came along when Mom was eleven. Big Jim, their gentle giant Newfoundland, used to pull Phyllis in a tiny cart.

Mom grew up where there was a community of friends and relatives who were always willing to help each other get the crops in on time. When they finished the hard work on the farm, there were dances and card games.

But Mom didn't want to stay on the farm or live in a small town, so when she was twenty-one, she moved to California to stay with an aunt and uncle who lived in an apartment above the carousel on the Santa Monica Pier. There were black-and-white glossy photos of her standing in front of her first car, a Ford. She was twenty-two years old in 1937 and on her first trip back to Illinois from California.

When I rummaged through the memory drawer, I found pictures of Mom in California. She posed with her best friend, Blanche, in huge sombreros during a trip to Tijuana. Mom always held a cigarette, looking like a sophisticated movie actress. She worked in Westwood as a secretary for a medical doctor. And she went dancing at the Aragon Ballroom or the Casino on Catalina Island. Her life felt as real to me as my own. Even now, decades later, I feel nostalgic for a time before I was born.

My dad's life wasn't as vivid to me. There weren't nearly as many photographs. My Mom couldn't share the feeling and flavor of his life because they weren't her memories, but she shared the details. My Dad, Jim, grew up in Chicago. He was two years old, the youngest of three boys, when his father, an attorney with political aspirations, died. Mom said the death seemed to be shrouded in mystery, although the official story was that my grandfather slipped on ice. Dad and his family weren't ones to talk about personal issues. Nora, his mother, raised her sons alone, supplementing her widow's pension by renting rooms to boarders. Having been raised by a rigid widower father who had little time for her, Nora had a limited repertoire of mothering skills.

Dad was the rascal of the family—a troublemaker who was always provoking the ire of the nuns at school. Drinking and fighting at a young age were common in his Irish neighborhood. But he was smart and did very well academically.

Dad and his brothers enlisted in the military after the attack on Pearl Harbor in 1941. John, the oldest, joined the Army and served in Europe. Joe was an Air Force pilot and became a

POW in Germany. My dad served in the Marine Corps. I loved the 8 x 10 picture of him in his Marine Corps uniform—a young man of twenty-three, his dark hair neatly combed back, an easy smile. The black-and-white photograph was tinted with a bit of color, as was the style in those days.

He was injured while fighting on Guadalcanal—shrapnel in his neck—and received a Purple Heart.

Back in the memory drawer, there were strips of one-inch pictures taken in a ten-cent photo booth on the Santa Monica Pier. Some of them were of Mom and Dad, smiling for the camera or gazing at each other.

I always looked for the picture of my parents taken on the day they were married. They sat close together on the steps of their home, smiling for the camera. The photo was black and white but I knew Mom's dress was blue with an ivory lace bodice because it had since been hanging in our hall closet. My parents hadn't known each other long when they married. I often asked Mom to tell me the story of the night they met.

It was 1943. The United States was fighting World War II in the Pacific and Europe. Mom was twenty-eight and Dad was twenty-four. He was on leave from the Naval Hospital in San Diego. In addition to his combat wound, he had contracted a severe case of malaria as well as tuberculosis. He and his friend Red set out for Santa Monica for a night out. They were happy to be alive and glad to be back in the USA. After growing up in Chicago's harsh climate, California seemed like heaven.

As my mother remembered that night, I imagined how the Miramar Ballroom in Santa Monica must have looked, charged with energy, smoke wafting above linen-covered tables; the hardwood dance floor gleaming with the light cast by crystal chandeliers; cocktail glasses clinking; and laughter rising above the sounds of the big bands. Dozens of couples would have been dancing to the music of Tommy Dorsey. With the help of a little beer, my dad was outgoing, not brash but friendly, funny, and smart. Mom said they danced and talked and laughed that first

night. They had a wonderful time, and at sunrise when he had to return to San Diego, they made plans to meet again.

While they waited for Dad's next leave, they wrote letters and discovered that they had a lot in common: They were both intelligent, loved books, and were from the Midwest. He was smitten. She felt the same.

The next time Dad came to visit, he met Mom's aunt and uncle. They were warm and welcoming, and he fit right in. They discussed the war, played card games like whist and euchre, told jokes, and spoke of hailing from Illinois and of their enchantment with California.

Mom told me that everyone knew someone who had been killed, captured, or injured in combat. One of her best friends from back home, Harold, died when the Japanese sank his ship. The sacrifices at home, like rationing, were made willingly, everyone knowing they paled against those of the soldiers.

Dad's diagnosis of tuberculosis meant a medical discharge from the Marine Corps, and he returned to his home in Chicago. He kept his promise to write to Mom. After six months, he proposed and she accepted. She later joked that she thought the beer in her refrigerator and the warm California climate inspired him to ask her.

When I was older I learned more. In the beginning, their marriage was easy. They drove to Illinois so Dad could meet her folks. Once again, he was welcomed with open arms. After a hard day's work on the farm, Mom's parents, Earl and Dora, joined Dad, Mom, and her brother Don for cards. Dad loved being part of her family. They liked him, too.

There was a little picture in the bottom of the memory drawer from a photo strip. It was of a woman with dark curly hair and dark lipstick. I'm not sure how old I was when Mom told me that she was someone with whom my father had been unfaithful. It was early in their marriage. Mom discovered hairpins in their bed. I don't think she ever forgave him. Why else would she keep the picture? She kept pictures of her old boyfriend, too. Bill was handsome, standing next to his convertible. I think he was the love of her life.

Over time, Mom realized that perhaps she didn't have so much in common with my dad after all. Mom worked at the Veteran's Administration as a secretary. Dad's work wasn't steady, and Mom thought he wasn't ambitious. She wanted to go out, socialize with friends, and talk about books. "When I met your Dad, we had books in common," she said. "I never thought he would never pick up a book again." Dad was content to listen to the radio and drink beer. Mom wanted to cook creative and interesting dishes like soufflés or special desserts. He preferred meat and potatoes. I never heard my father's version of those years. He kept his memories more to himself.

Mom became increasingly unhappy. Dad may not have truly understood her unrest. He was content; why wasn't she?

After seven years, with no children or intimacy to keep her, they separated. I don't know if they wanted children or not, but they had taken no measures to prevent it.

One year later, Mom's mother was engulfed in flames when a spark ignited gasoline she was using to clean some farm equipment. My grandmother dropped to the ground, rolling in the dirt. Earl came when he heard her screams, but the burns were extensive. The closest hospital was small and ill-equipped to treat her, so she was transferred to Chicago.

Mom and her sister Phyllis went immediately to Illinois to be with their mother. Day after day, stoic and strong, Mom held her mother's hand while nurses scrubbed the burns. Dora's pain was excruciating. When Mom saw that her mother's urine output was dwindling, she brought it to the nurses' attention. "Don't worry, honey, we're taking good care of her," they said. When Dora became feverish after blood transfusions, Mom asked the doctor what was wrong. Again, she received a patronizing response. After seven weeks of suffering, Dora passed away.

Mom didn't tell me in so many words how devastated she was by her loss, but I came to understand how lonely she felt without her mother. When Mom returned to California, she spent some time with Dad. He had been close to Dora, too. Their time together would most likely have been limited. They would have probably separated again and eventually divorced, but Mom discovered that she was pregnant. This changed everything.

preemie

Michele Colleen Sullivan, Mikey, was a fragile baby born into a fragile marriage. She weighed 2.3 pounds when she entered the world on February 2, 1953, and went directly into an incubator.

Mom told me the story of those early days. My parents stood by helplessly as Mikey fought to live. They weren't allowed to touch her. The nurses didn't touch her either—only when absolutely necessary. That was the way things were done then.

Mom's time working at the VA gave her access to medical journals, and she researched whatever she could find about premature babies. She found a study that showed that too much oxygen can cause blindness and brought it to Mikey's doctor. If the doctor ordered correct levels, at least one nurse sabotaged them. Mom told me about the nurse who said, "No baby is going to die on my shift," as she cranked the oxygen all the way up. Mikey was in an incubator for weeks and stayed in the hospital for several more before she was strong enough to go home.

It wasn't until after she left the hospital that doctors diagnosed her with retrolental fibroplasia—complete destruction of her retina, total blindness.

My parents remained optimistic. Of course, Mikey's blindness would present challenges, but she would have a nearly normal life.

In those first months, she suffered. She rubbed her eyes, constantly cried, and seldom slept. My father walked for hours, cradling her in his arms, trying to comfort her. He lost thirty pounds in two months.

Shortly after Mikey was born, my mother's obstetrician told my parents that if they wanted a "normal" baby, they should have one right away. My parents didn't think of Mikey as abnormal. The doctor was referring to my mother's age. Thirty-eight was considered old for having babies.

I was born thirteen months after Mikey. I was a little girl when my mother told me about the doctor's recommendation. I'd like to think she wanted me to know that I was special and wanted, but by that time Mikey's handicaps made it clear that I was probably more of a burden than a blessing. In my little girl's mind, I understood her to say that I was born for the purpose of making our family normal. I felt that along with the designation of "normal" came great responsibility and obligation.

When she was two years old, Mikey underwent surgery for glaucoma. She had the kind of glaucoma that was painful. My mother insisted that Dad stay at the hospital with Mikey while she was at home with me, but parents couldn't remain after visiting hours. The nuns insisted that my father go home, and he complied. Mom told me later that she thought he didn't stand up to the nuns because, as a child in Catholic school, he had been firmly indoctrinated never to question them. Poor Mikey was all alone in an unfamiliar place, surrounded by unfamiliar sounds, poked and prodded by strangers, and in pain. One of the nurses told my mother and father that Mikey cried all night long. My mother thought that there might have been a dripping faucet during that night because for years, whenever Mikey heard dripping water, she panicked and cried. After the eye surgery, she developed painful iritis. Then she had a second surgery because the first operation had been unsuccessful.

Mikey spoke early and developed typically. She liked big

words like "rambunctious" and said, "baby cry, baby cry" when I cried. She joined in when my parents sang nursery rhymes and clapped her hands to patty-cake. She navigated easily, instinctively walking with her arms outstretched to avoid obstacles she could not see.

When she was two-and-a-half years old, everything changed.

One moment she would be mimicking nursery rhymes, the next she started screaming and clutching her feet. She became progressively withdrawn, stopped speaking and resisted all attempts to hold or comfort her.

She didn't respond to sound and seemed to be deaf.

When I was older and Mom described this time to me, she said, "I watched her drop something heavy on her foot. It must have hurt, but she just stood there. She didn't react at all, didn't withdraw her foot, didn't grimace or cry. After almost a minute, she screamed and bit herself."

My parents took her to see pediatricians, neurologists, and psychologists. Child development specialists evaluated her. Audiologists tested her hearing. Her brain waves were measured. It was impossible to measure her cognitive ability due to her complete lack of response.

My parents wondered if the sensory deprivation of her time in the incubator had caused her withdrawal. Studies since then have shown that it is critical for premature babies to be touched and held. Maybe the pain, fear, and isolation she experienced during her time in the hospital when she had eye surgery contributed to the withdrawal. Maybe a virus was the cause. Perhaps her prematurity—therefore, a lack of brain development—was to blame. But she had developed typically until it all stopped. Could it be the excessive oxygen that had also blinded her?

Finally, a neurologist named Dr. Sedgewick said, "My God, this child is profoundly brain-damaged. Why hasn't she been institutionalized?" Mom said that it was a relief to know what was wrong, even if they didn't know why. It wasn't until decades later that research suggested that extremely low birth weight (ELBW) affects brain development and that these children were at greater risk for autism.

Over the next couple of years, as I developed typically, Mikey gradually re-joined the world—but never completely. She began to respond to sounds, but she didn't speak. If my parents sang patty-cake, she raised her hands as if to clap but stopped with her hands in mid-air. It was as if the wiring in her brain had short-circuited. My parents understood or misunderstood her by her vocalizations and gestures: reaching out, moans, smiles, giggles, grimaces, whimpers, sometimes bites and scratches. As I grew older, I learned her language too.

Some of her behaviors seemed to signal that she might be in pain, like banging her head on the wall. But my parents could seldom be certain. They thought her eyes could be causing her to suffer. She rubbed them a lot and winced when bright sun shone on her. But the doctors said no, it couldn't be her eyes. I don't know if she understood the question, "Where does it hurt?" She couldn't say yes or no. She couldn't point or otherwise indicate where her pain was—if she was in pain. My parents looked in her mouth, pressed on her abdomen and watched for a flinch, or held a cool cloth to her eyes and waited to see if she calmed down.

By the time she was six, Mikey's re-emergence had plateaued. She grew physically, but developmentally remained about two years old. We could never know her interior life. Is it possible that she was more typical than she appeared but couldn't communicate?

Over the ensuing years, children like Mikey were given many different labels that varied by year and reflected the credentials of the professional making the diagnosis. Childhood schizophrenia was a popular diagnosis in the 1950s. It referred to symptoms now associated with autism, such as loss of speech and inability to bond or relate socially. Psychiatrists postulated that "refrigerator mothers" who deprived their children of love and affection caused the syndrome. Another label was "mentally retarded," which was divided into two groups. "Trainable mentally retarded" referred to those children who might be able to master simple functions, such as using the toilet or utensils. "Educable mentally retarded" described higher-functioning children able to learn more advanced skills, such as speaking in sentences. "Developmentally disabled" was a term used much later. We always referred to her as brain-damaged. Back then, the label made no difference. The treatment was the same: Nothing. And, frequently, institutionalization.

Sometimes, children like Mikey were referred to as "exceptional." It sounds nice, doesn't it? Families like mine might be labeled as exceptional families. Does that mean I was an "exceptional sister?"

early years

I was born in the middle of the baby boom, in 1954, so there were a lot of kids on our block. We went to each other's homes for birthday parties, where we played Pin the Tail on the Donkey, ate birthday cake, and opened presents. The other kids didn't seem to notice or care about Mikey. In the years before I started school, she was mostly rocking and spinning, hyperactive but not as disruptive as she later became, and not biting very much yet. But if she was having a bad day, I went to a friend's house.

Dad had taken a training course at Hoffman Television, and he continued to work there after he completed his classes. I'm not sure what he did exactly. Sometimes he repaired TVs on the side. Mom stayed at home. I didn't realize that she had to stretch paychecks. I always had nice clothes, and I never thought twice about some of those clothes coming from a thrift shop.

Most days, my friend Connie's mom, Liz, came over from across the street to have a cup of tea with Mom. When Mikey was small, before everything went wrong, Liz would bounce her on her knee and coo and tickle her. Even after Mikey changed, Liz came over to visit. Mom told me when I was a little older how much it meant to her when someone showed affection toward

Mikey. Other days Mom took us to my Aunt Phyllis's house. I think she hoped that spending time with my cousins Johnny and Jimmy would give me an experience similar to having typical siblings. The visits also gave my mother another chance to spend time with an adult, although my aunt always seemed annoyed by Mikey.

We knew one other family like ours—Tom, Kay, and their son Johnny, who was Mikey's age. Johnny had also been blinded in the incubator, didn't speak, and was sometimes violent. Some days, Mom, Mikey, and I went to an outdoor restaurant to meet Johnny and his mom. It was a good day if both Mikey and Johnny were manageable enough for everyone to have a little lunch.

I hadn't started kindergarten yet the first time we went to a Christmas party, thrown by a couple in Santa Monica, that became an annual tradition. It was just for blind children and their families, and the crowd filled a large auditorium colorfully decorated with crepe paper. Christmas music played and the tree, hung with green and red ornaments and lots of silver tinsel, was taller than any I had ever seen. There were dozens of wrapped presents underneath.

We sat with Johnny and his family, and Mikey was having a good time. She rocked to the music and licked frosting off her fingers, seeming to sense the happy atmosphere. Santa Claus came onto the stage with Mrs. Claus, and Mikey giggled when his deep voice bellowed into the microphone, "Ho, Ho, Ho. Merry Christmas. Is everyone ready for presents?"

"Yes!" the children called out.

Mrs. Claus picked a present, one at a time, from under the tree and brought it to Santa. He called out a name.

"Here! Here!" a young child across the room called out, raising his arm high in the air. An elf, in a green costume with a jester's hat, brought the gift to the child. The parents raised their hands for the children who couldn't.

"Terry Sullivan!" Santa called out. I almost jumped out of my seat with surprise and delight. I strained to raise my arm as high as I could. "Here!" I opened the package to find a small cloth doll with blond ringlets.

I think of that couple, Santa and his wife, fondly. They were so thoughtful to give presents to siblings as well as the blind children.

When we went home, our own tree was specially decorated—no fragile ornaments, lots of tinsel, and brightly-colored twinkling lights—and placed, as it was every year, in the corner of the living room where it wouldn't interfere with Mikey's path. Once she knew where the tree was, there was no danger that she would bump into it.

I recall that Christmas, when I was five, vividly. It was early morning when I came into the living room. I was still in my pajamas. We had exchanged small presents with Aunt Phyllis's family on Christmas Eve, but I got my main present on Christmas morning. My gifts that year were too large to wrap. I saw her as soon as I rounded the corner into the living room. "Oh boy, Patty Play Pal!" A three-foot doll with curly red hair, wearing a blue-and-white-striped dress with a black bow at the neck, and patent shoes with white bobby socks, sat in a child-size white Naugahyde rocking chair, my other present.

I wasn't normally interested in dolls, but this was a little girl, not a baby, and the best present ever! After positioning her just right in her rocking chair, I turned to tell Mom and Dad, "She's just what I wanted!"

Within ten minutes, Mikey found Patty and pulled her arm out of its socket. It only took her a moment. Dad turned when he heard her giggle, but it was too late. He took the doll away from Mikey and examined the damage, but Patty was broken beyond repair.

Armless Patty was put away in the garage and forgotten for years.

Tears welled in my eyes, but I didn't complain. Mom said, "I'm sorry, honey," and we continued on with our morning. I sat in my new little girl's rocking chair and opened some small presents. I don't remember what they were.

Did Mikey do it because she was jealous? Sometimes she got agitated when I was getting attention. Or was she attracted by the commotion and discovered Patty when she was feeling around, intrigued by an unusual object to manipulate?

Only now do I wonder why my parents didn't replace the doll. Maybe there wasn't enough money. If I had cried openly or protested more, would they have responded differently? But I was quietly resigned. I understood, not only because my parents explained it to me, but also because I intuitively knew that Mikey couldn't help the way she was. Dad once said, "Mikey will go to heaven because she is innocent." He explained that she didn't know the difference between good and evil, that she was guileless and pure. This belief probably came from his Catholic upbringing.

I can't help but think that, deep inside, I was frustrated when Mikey destroyed my belongings and hurt when Mom gave me a stern look and shushed me if I spoke at the wrong time, upsetting Mikey.

When I was a little older, Mom tried to comfort me by saying, "It's okay to be angry." She may have thought I was too good. I think she worried that I resented Mikey and that I might eventually retaliate.

When I was in my twenties, Dad shared his remorse for the sacrifices I'd made. He told me that I had been a perfect child and was "basically ignored." But that was my normal. I found security in feeling that I brought relief and value by helping, understanding, and by not needing too much when my parents were clearly stretched too thin. I didn't want to disappoint them.

Dad told me about the time he came home from work when Mikey and I were very little, barely toddlers. I ran to him, "Daddy! Daddy!" and he scooped me up, nuzzling my neck while I giggled because it tickled. Seconds later Mikey stood at his feet and he put me down to pick her up. I shed silent tears. My moment with my Daddy was cut short as he turned his full attention to her. "We made a decision that we had to give the most to the one who needed the most," he said. "I think we might have made the wrong decision." I believe he suffered more than I did for the sacrifices I made. It was all I had ever known. I didn't wonder how things could have been different.

My life away from home was normal. I liked to escape to Karen Olsen's house for dinner. She had freckles and red hair that she wore in braids and three older sisters. They lived five houses up the block. I especially liked to visit when they had leftovers. Jasper, the dachshund, lived there. Karen and I rode our bikes, skipped rope, and made mud pies together.

I wore a pink and blue pastel sleeveless dress on the first day of kindergarten at Grant Elementary School and joined the other children to play on the jungle gym in the playground. Mikey couldn't go to school. There weren't any special classes or services for children like her.

I took tap dancing and baton lessons at Brownie Brown's dance school. Our uniforms featured a gold emblem on the chest and were complemented by a gold hat, and we marched in the local Fourth of July parade. There were other baton groups and a band that marched behind us, and pretty horses too. I stood up straight and held my baton just right when I saw Mom and Dad standing in the crowd watching me. Mikey was sitting on my Dad's shoulders. I joined the Brownies in the second grade, played a pilgrim in the school Thanksgiving play, and sang in the church choir.

We went to Mount Olive Lutheran Church on Sundays, Easter, and Christmas. Although Dad had been raised Catholic, he didn't mind going to the Lutheran church. He liked Pastor Hoff, who had been a chaplain in the Marine Corps during World War II.

Gradually, neighbors who knew us when Mikey was younger and easier moved away. Newer neighbors waved when we drove by, or fathers chatted when they took a break from mowing lawns, but I don't remember any of them coming over. I don't know if it was because we didn't invite them or because they preferred not to be around Mikey.

As time passed, I became more aware of the contrast between my life at home and my life at school. I often crossed the bridge between worlds alone. I didn't invite just anyone home. I paid attention. I noticed if children called someone "retarded" to belittle or hurt. I didn't want their friendship. I listened when people told Helen Keller jokes, but I didn't laugh, and I didn't invite them home either. Their comments weren't directed at Mikey or me. They didn't know about her. Only my friends knew. I think those of us from "different" families develop a sixth sense about who will be kind toward our vulnerable children or siblings. We can tell who will shy away from us once they see our "weird" family member.

I'm sure my caution and selectivity grew as much from my need to protect myself from cruelty as from my desire to shield Mikey.

anne

I was eight years old and it was the first day of third grade when I met Anne. I had seen her before, but we had been in different classes in the second grade.

We were in the midst of a heat wave. Santa Ana winds blew hot air from the east, sending brittle leaves skittering across the asphalt and driving all clouds from the pale blue sky. First recess had just begun, and I sat on a wood bench in the schoolyard. The slats were almost too hot against my bare legs.

Girls gathered in clusters or dashed to play a quick game of hopscotch. Boys punched each other's biceps, the puncher and punched each demonstrating their toughness in front of their peers. The playground was loud with the sound of children laughing and hollering.

I noticed Anne standing alone under a scrawny shade tree in a faded blue cotton dress that hung loosely on her slight frame. She had skinny legs, knobby knees, and wore saddle shoes with white bobby socks that sagged around her ankles. Thin, wavy blond hair framed her face. She looked uneasy standing there with her head bowed, squinting against the sun, peeking out through her glasses. Then I realized that she was wearing new glasses. New glasses! I was sure of it. Brown plastic frames, almost, but not quite, too large for her face. Now I knew why she stood alone. If I were in her shoes, I would avoid the other children too. Once they spotted her, they would begin jeering "four eyes" and telling her she was "the ugliest girl in school" until she gave them what they wanted: tears. Maybe I felt sympathy for her because I understood her vulnerability. I instinctively felt the same protectiveness for her that I felt for Mikey.

When the bell rang, signaling the end of recess, Anne trailed behind the other students. I waited too. As I passed her on the way back to class, I said "Hi."

She looked up. "Hi."

A friendship that would shape my life had begun.

At lunch, I saw her standing alone again. Her hands were clasped behind her back, and she looked like she was watching for something or someone. Was she waiting for me?

I approached and said, "I like your glasses." I was sure she hated them.

She was a little shorter than me and when she looked up to meet my eyes, I noticed that hers were sky blue, the same color as my mother's.

"Really? I just got them." She sounded hopeful.

"Yeah, they look good. Do you want to have lunch?" I asked.

"Okay." The ice was broken. The momentary uncertainty of acceptance or rejection was behind us, and we headed to the cafeteria. I had quarters for the usual mac-and-cheese, sandwich, and a mini-carton of milk. Anne carried a brown paper sack from home.

That day Anne survived lunch and another recess with an ally by her side. The shield we had already begun to construct deflected the few taunts from other children.

Within no time at all, we spent every recess and lunch together. We usually sat alone in the farthest part of the playground on our bench next to the chain link fence. Other children lined up a short distance away at the ball box or played games on the playground.

Sometimes, when we were at our spot in the far reaches of the playground, we looked up at the sky. Because our lunchtimes were uncluttered by the distraction of groups and games, we were convinced that we were the only ones who noticed the words and numbers that pilots were writing with vapor trails from their jets. The messages faded quickly as the vapor dissipated. We decided that the writing in the sky was a secret code that the pilots used to communicate with each other. Douglas Aircraft was a half block from my house and a mile from the school. I explained that my Mom had told me it had been a target during World War II. Now we were in a cold war with Russia and the threat of nuclear attack was real for all Americans. The proximity of Douglas led us to think that we were in greater danger.

Our teachers had shown us a film to prepare us for the bomb that Russia might drop at any moment. On the first Friday of every month, the sirens blared throughout the city, and we scrambled under our little desks to "duck and cover." We covered our heads and squeezed our eyes shut so that the nuclear flash wouldn't blind us and glass from exploding windows wouldn't cut us. Many of us had seen pictures of Hiroshima, and we knew that that Los Angeles would be destroyed if Russia dropped a bomb. We would be incinerated.

Sometimes during our lunchtime discussions Anne and I took turns talking about our aches and pains. "I had a sharp stab in my stomach last night. About an eight," Anne would say. We used a one-to-ten scale. "That's terrible," I responded with concern. "How long did it last?"

"Almost an hour."

Our pains always came at night, alone in our beds.

"Mine wasn't so bad," I said. "My leg was throbbing—about a four."

"Probably your bones growing."

There was nothing wrong with either of us. I think we did it because the sympathy felt so nice. Together, it was okay to get attention for our little hurts.

I learned about Anne's family. She was the second of four girls. Her big sister was two years older—a big gap when you're eight years old. Her other two sisters were quite a bit younger. I think that Anne was a little lost in the middle of her family. I explained about Mikey. With parents stretched so thin and without a typical sibling, I was a bit lost, too. We had aloneness in common.

After school, we sometimes walked to her house, which was right next door. All four sisters shared a small bedroom. A pair of bunk beds left only a few feet of open space. Other times we walked the twenty minutes to my house, where we had my bedroom all to ourselves. Mikey was banned and, for the most part, she stayed out, so the room was fairly neat. There was no food on the walls—I even had floral wallpaper. I had a blond highboy dresser, shelves that held lots of books, and a small record player. Here, Anne and I talked about what was important to nine-year-old girls in 1963: The Beatles. Every girl had her favorite. George, the quiet one, was Anne's, and Paul, the cute one, was mine. We played 45 rpm records on my little phonograph and sang along to "I Want to Hold Your Hand", bobbing our heads in time to the beat. We practiced dancing the twist to John Lennon singing "Twist and Shout" and talked about what we would wear to the lunchtime dance on Friday afternoons in the school auditorium.

Anne rescued me just as much as I rescued her. My friendship with her gave me courage. We were braver together. We had a connection that would sometimes have grave implications as we grew older.

trips

Dad bolted metal latches to the exterior of each door on our station wagon so that we could lock them from the outside. Mikey loved riding in the car and often pulled the hand of any one of us to tug us toward the front door. We used the station wagon to calm her down when she was agitated. The steady feeling of movement seemed to soothe her. If a window was open, she held still to feel the breeze on her face. Music played on the radio. Mikey liked music with a beat, and she rocked rhythmically, sometimes giggling for no apparent reason. Sometimes we all piled in the car for a wandering half-hour drive with no particular destination.

Mikey usually sat in the far back so she wouldn't jeopardize the driver if she reached out and grabbed hair or tried to get out. A second person was always along to maintain order.

It would have been impossible to take her in the car without the latches because sometimes she tried to open the doors, whether we were stopped or traveling fifty miles per hour in traffic.

Drive-in restaurants gave us a way to go out for a meal without being too disruptive to others. Goody Goody was our favorite. Mikey perked up when the waitress affixed trays filled with hamburgers, French fries, fish sandwiches, and milkshakes to the car windows. The delicious aroma meant something good was coming.

Often the people parked next to us watched from their cars, ignoring their food and staring, transfixed by Mikey. Sometimes they stood right next to us and peered in the windows. They didn't look at my parents or me—they couldn't take their eyes off Mikey. I resented that they didn't respect our privacy, that they didn't see her as a person but as a freak. Of course I didn't know what they thought or how they felt. The kind explanations that my parents offered, that people were just curious or didn't realize that they were staring, didn't appease me. I simmered silently.

We went out of our way not to disrupt the lives of "normal" families. Occasionally, we tried a real restaurant, as long as we could sit away from the other patrons. Pickle Bill's was casual, with wood picnic benches and sawdust on the floor, so dropping a little food didn't seem like a big deal. At least the owners or employees didn't appear to be bothered. Customers ordered their sandwiches at a counter in the front and picked up their food, so there weren't many employees. They ignored us for the most part. Sometimes they even smiled when we came in. We always cleaned up any spilled food before we left.

My parents wanted Mikey to fit into the real world as much as possible. They had tried and tried to teach her to use utensils, but she had to use her fingers to find and identify the food on her plate then push it onto her fork. Telling her that there were "potatoes at nine o'clock" meant nothing. Forked food often fell before it reached her mouth; she was more successful with a spoon, especially with one of us guiding her hand. Adequate nourishment and quality of life trumped etiquette.

Sometimes we took a trip with Mikey to the produce department at the grocery store. Her face lit up when she felt the different shapes and textures of fruit on display. She was careful as she reached out, picking up an orange and delicately feeling the dimpled skin. She held it to her nose to smell the fruity perfume.

Then she held it out for us to take. Of course, the lookers were here, too.

During one trip to the market, when I was about eight, a mother and her children were watching us. They stood slack-jawed in the aisle about ten feet away. The two young boys, perhaps seven or eight years old, were whispering and pointing at Mikey. The strange girl with sunken eyes was rocking and making odd noises as she reached her arm out, searching. Most days, I just ignored the stares, but that day I was particularly annoyed. Was I embarrassed? I took a wide-based stance, all four feet of me. With my hands on my hips, I stared intensely back at them, sending a silent, hostile message: "What does it feel like to be stared at? Don't you have any manners?" I might as well have been invisible. After a few moments, the mother pulled the children away, maybe feeling grateful that she didn't have such a child, and maybe a little afraid. We continued, Mikey holding onto the cart handle, rocking and smiling. As I look back, I realize that I never saw other children like Mikey in public. Many were in institutions, and perhaps the families who kept them home chose not to venture into the outside world.

We went to the Olympic Drive-in movie theater and saw Disney movies. There was a small playground below the screen and before the movie started, Mikey rode on the swings. Dad bought buttered popcorn and hot dogs at the concession. Mikey couldn't understand movies, but sometimes she giggled at the odd voices of the characters, like Elmer Fudd and his "Silly wab-bit." Sometimes she slept. We often brought a baby-bottle of milk with a little molasses in it. Typical children her age would be too old for a bottle, but Mikey was content to suck on the nipple. We went to Arlene's Donut Shop at midnight to get fresh, hot donuts that we ate in the car.

We took overnight trips, too. We always left late at night, when Mikey was calmer and traffic lighter.

One night we set out for Las Vegas. The aluminum cooler sat on the front seat between my mom and dad. Mom had filled it with ice cubes, little bottles of grape juice, and bologna sand-wiches. She had a paper sack of treats for Mikey—Nilla wafers and chocolate mint candies. There were blankets in case Mikey and I slept. We pulled a small travel trailer behind the station wagon, a blue-and-white Westerner. Mom had put a few West-ern-style decals of cowboys and stagecoaches on the honey-col-ored wood inside. We were stocked with whatever we needed for a couple of days.

My aunt Phyllis and her children, John, Jim, and Cathy, had left earlier in the day, pulling their travel trailer. We were going to meet them at the trailer park where we would all stay.

As we drove off, around midnight, most of the houses on our block were dark. I stayed awake as long as I could, lean-ing over the front seat between my parents. The speedometer illuminated my father's face as he drove; his wrist was hanging loosely over the steering wheel. Mom's cigarette glowed bright red when she took a puff. Mikey masturbated quietly in the far back, lying on her stomach. It was quiet. I was happy we were all together. Driving through the desert, it seemed like we traveled hours without seeing another car. The only illumination was our headlights illuminating a stretch of black asphalt. Occasional tumbleweeds swept across the road.

The next thing I knew, Mom was shaking me gently. I had fallen asleep, curled up in a blanket on the back seat. It was still dark outside when Dad carried me into the trailer, where Mikey was already settled in a bed that converted into a dinette during the day.

In the morning, Phyllis made coffee for the grown ups and we children had cereal and milk while sitting at a picnic table. There were other children our age and a small playground in the park. My parents worked out a system where one could go out, maybe to a casino, while the other stayed at the trailer with the kids.

I loved car trips as much as Mikey did, loved being with my family, loved the close quarters, and loved the adventure.

placement

Resources for people like Mikey were almost non-existent in the 1960s. Because of the severity of her handicaps, Mikey would require much more attention than the higher-functioning children.

Shortly after the severity of Mikey's impairments became evident, doctors suggested that my parents "place" her. Placement meant living away from home. But my parents resisted. They hoped they would find help and that she could get better.

When she was nine, we were hopeful when a nice lady let Mikey come to her classes for retarded children at a nearby Baptist church. Her name was Mrs. Washington. She was a large black woman who wore dark dresses and "sensible" shoes. I could sense the strength of her personality—confident and in charge, but also warm and loving. She was kind to my mom.

Classes consisted of activities designed to stimulate and occupy the children, like putting a round block of wood into a round hole instead of the square hole. Mikey was good at that kind of task and enjoyed the accomplishment.

Three days a week, after Mom picked me up from school, we drove to the church to pick up Mikey. One day, after Mikey had been attending classes for two weeks, Mrs. Washington walked toward us in the parking lot just as we were getting out of the car.

"I am so very sorry, Mrs. Sullivan," she said. "I can't allow Michele to continue in our classes. She attacked another child today."

She went on to tell us that Mikey had reached out and grabbed the hair of a little girl. The girl was not injured, and the staff had removed Mikey to another room right away. She told us about Mikey's unmanageable tirade, which had lasted for another half hour.

"I know we were both concerned that this might happen, and I prayed that it wouldn't come to this, but I cannot endanger my other pupils," Mrs. Washington said. She didn't seem to be mad at Mikey, and I think she felt sorry for us. She opened her arms a little, like she was going to hug Mom, but Mom stood stiffly. Mrs. Washington was so warm and kind. I would have liked to be hugged by her, held tightly against her chest and comforted.

"Institutionalization" was a kind of placement, and Pacific State Hospital was where mentally retarded children were sent. I reflect now on how my parents must have struggled with their dilemma: to keep Mikey home or to institutionalize her. It was abundantly clear that she would never be able to join the "real" world. She would always need someone to care for all her basic needs. She would forever be two years old. My parents were smart, practical, and kind people. There were no guidelines for a child so disabled as Mikey. Maybe they hoped that she could be helped in an institution and perhaps have a happier life. Did they believe that it was better to commit her sooner than later, making it easier for everyone to adjust? Who would benefit and who would be harmed by such an upheaval?

I didn't realize at the time that their marriage was strained. Perhaps if they had been free from the demands of caring for Mikey, they would have separated. Or maybe they would have had a better marriage. If they fought about it, I never heard a harsh word between them. I never heard discussions about Mikey's destiny. I wonder if they cried.

I'm sure they were worried about what would happen to her when they were old, or after they died. Did they think that I would not, could not, or should not have to continue to care for her? Perhaps they hoped that sending Mikey away would provide me with a more normal childhood.

When Mikey was nine years old, she went to Pacific State Hospital. Mom told me how her brief stay unfolded, and it inspired me to write my first story about Mikey, in pencil on both sides of a sheet of beige construction paper, when I was eight years old.

Mom and Dad took Mikey to Pacific State Hospital. She had to stay in isolation for three days. Mom and Dad could watch her through the glass, but they weren't allowed to talk to her. She was alone in a glass room, and it was hot, and she was thirsty, but no one gave her anything to drink. She reached out her arm, but no one came. The people at the hospital told my mom and dad that Mikey had to learn that her parents weren't going to take care of her anymore. After three days, Mom couldn't stand to leave her there, so they brought her home.

Dad told me years later how deeply he respected and admired my mother for refusing to allow Mikey to remain at Pacific State.

One day we visited a place called Home of the Guiding Hands. It was a Catholic residential program for disabled children, with a more home-like environment. My parents hoped Mikey could get some personal attention there. It would cost money, and there was none to spare, but that was a bridge my parents would cross if Mikey was accepted.

It was a warm, sunny day in summer when we all set out for our interview and tour. The home was about ninety miles north of Los Angeles, in a pastoral setting near Santa Barbara. A nun wearing a habit led us to a cool, grassy courtyard where small clusters of five or six young children, about fifteen in all, sat at picnic tables. Female staff members at each table, not wearing habits, supervised and helped the children eat lunch, feeding some, encouraging others.

Mom, Dad, and Mikey went to meet with the head nun in her office for an interview while I sat near a pond and watched dragonflies and a frog in the warm sunshine. On the drive up, Mikey had seemed calm and happy, smiling and rocking gently. Like my parents, I hoped her mood would last, and she would make a good impression, and that the nun would see the vulnerable child beneath her destructive behavior. Maybe the nun would find it in her heart to accept Mikey. Hopefully, she would see her potential and rise to the challenge. My mother told me later that Mikey was perfect that day. She stayed seated, smiled, and rocked. But she was rejected because she had "multiple handicaps." I don't know why the nun met with my parents. She knew what Mikey's handicaps were before we arrived. She must have already known what her answer would be. Maybe she thought it was the Christian thing to do—be kind to the poor parents. But she pulled the chair out from under them, offering hope and snatching it away.

As they walked toward me after the interview, Dad was holding Mikey's hand. The nun pulled Mom aside for a minute. On the way home, Mom told Dad that the nun said to her: "The Lord fits the burden to the shoulders." I heard the sarcasm in Mom's voice when she said, "I told her, I think He overestimated mine." She wasn't buying the "this is God's will" explanation and found no comfort in it. Even then I understood how she would find this reassurance empty.

I think that there were times, though, when my parents found a little comfort in believing that God sent them such a challenge because they were good people and worthy of being charged with loving and caring for Mikey. But time after time their belief was tested.

In 1978, Josh Greenfield, the father of a boy whose handicaps were similar to Mikey's, published his journal, *A Place for Noah*. The entry he made after visiting an institution says: "I see no way out. I'm boxed into an untenable situation. We must keep Noah at home as long as we can, otherwise we destroy his life. But we cannot keep him at home too long, otherwise, we destroy our lives. Poor kid, it's him against us."

turkey

Our refrigerator was full of tastes and textures, and I often found Mikey sitting on the kitchen floor rummaging for delicacies. Tart canned cherries were a favorite. She often sat with the door propped open by her skinny body, the light from the fridge shining on her face. Then she picked one cherry at a time from the open can she held. She was obedient and cooperative when she wasn't having an explosion, so when I asked, she handed me the can and left the refrigerator.

To reduce the amount of food on the walls and floors, Dad finally moved the fridge into the garage to prevent Mikey's access. Once she discovered where it was, we began to lock the garage door.

On the day before Thanksgiving, when I was nine, I set out to make myself a sandwich. I climbed onto the kitchen counter to reach the top shelf of the cabinet where we hid the key to the garage door. I found it after feeling around, then climbed down, went out the back door, and down the porch steps. It was cool and dim in the garage, but there was enough light from the open door. Inside the refrigerator I found milk, orange juice, bread, an open can of cherries, bologna, and a medium-sized uncooked turkey. Onions and celery for the turkey stuffing were in the crisper. I pulled out sandwich makings then carefully locked up as usual and returned the key to its hiding place. This system had been in place for several months and was working well.

November days are short, and sunsets are often spectacular. That day, the color had faded from the sky and it was almost dark, which of course made no difference to Mikey. Mom stood at the kitchen sink looking out the window at our expansive backyard. There were no obstacles, no bushes or furniture, with the exception of a swing set that Mikey found easily and often. Watching her swing would probably be scary for the uninitiated. She was fearless. She looked as if she might swing all the way over the horizontal bar at the top. As she began her descent, her broad smile would become a gleeful laugh, and she would look like joy personified. But Mikey wasn't on the swing that evening. Dad and I heard Mom holler, "Come here! Look at this!" And we came running.

"What's wrong?" My dad was worried.

"Look!" she pointed.

We all stared out the window. Mikey was twirling fast. We could tell she was laughing.

"What's she got?" Dad asked.

In each hand, Mikey held a leg of our uncooked Thanksgiving turkey. Her extended arms and the speed of her spinning held the whole bird aloft.

We all laughed at her joy and her ingenuity and waited until she slowed to a stop before retrieving the turkey. She had listened carefully and waited until no one was near to get the hidden key so she could raid the refrigerator.

Mikey spent a lot of time twirling, usually in front of the hi-fi in the living room. "The Carrot Seed Song" or Alvin and the Chipmunks played for hours, uninterrupted, until someone changed the record. As the rest of us went about our day, the tune faded into the background, but the lyrics were forever imprinted on my subconscious.

In her wrinkled dress, her short brown hair matted with food, and a smile on her face, Mikey moved to the music's rhythm, sometimes fast, sometimes slow. Her bare feet slapped on the linoleum, and her arms swung as she laughed and made happy sounds. Sometimes she sat on the floor, her ear pressed against the speaker, entranced by the nearness of the sounds and the bass vibration.

Above the hi-fi, on the living room wall, hung a large painting of an older gentleman. He sat in a warmly paneled room at a table draped with a white cloth, holding a cup in one hand and a newspaper in the other. Snow was visible through the window behind him. We didn't know him—I think my mother bought the painting at an auction—but he was a comforting presence with his kind eyes and calm countenance.

The painting hangs in my dining room now, stained with beets and something tan that looks like mashed potatoes. I often sit at the table and enjoy a cup of tea with my old friend.

When I hear The Chipmunks singing "Christmas Don't be Late" (it's on my iPod), I feel a flutter in my chest. My response is bittersweet and automatic. A smile crosses my face as my muscles clench with grief. I recall the sweetness of Mikey's uninhibited joy, but her suffering always colors my memories. I think of our family, of home, of feeling close and safe because we were in it together. Then thoughts of the ensuing years intrude.

babysitting

Mom had started going out to play poker with her sister Phyllis when I was about eight. There were several card clubs in Gardena, about forty-five minutes south of us: the Monterey Club, the Normandie, and the Gardena Club. Mom always played at the Gardena Club.

Mom and I developed a ritual for the nights she went out. It began at around 8:30 P.M. If I was lucky, our time together would be uninterrupted by Mikey. In the mid-1960s, women still wore dresses most of the time. Hats and gloves were reserved for church. I leaned against the doorjamb watching as she sat on the edge of her bed to put on her nylons. The round elastic garters that she used to hold them up were like large cloth-covered rubber bands. I zipped up the back of her lucky green wool dress and followed her to the bathroom, where she discovered the cup of black tea that I often made to surprise her. Sometimes I brought her a bowl of walnuts. She had an inexplicable craving for them and often bought a couple dozen at the grocery store. I took ten or so out on the back porch and put one at a time in a kitchen towel. Crouching, I smashed the shell on the concrete with a hammer, trying not to hit too hard so I could remove the meat intact. When I brought them to her, setting the bowl on the bathroom counter, she seemed surprised and pleased. "Thank you, honey. These look wonderful."

Our bathroom was small, so I was only a couple of feet from her as I sat on the closed toilet seat and watched her fix her hair. Her natural color was light brown, but she started coloring it a light shade of red at about the same time she began going out. She twisted the gold lipstick tube, rolled up an inch of orange, and leaned close to the mirror to apply it to her thin lips; then she blotted them with a tissue. Next, she clipped on a pair of shimmering earrings that matched her dress. The room filled with a fine mist when she froze her hairdo with Aquanet hairspray. Some of it settled on my skin, and I pretended to be bothered, swiping the air to disperse it. She turned and smiled. The last step in the ritual that I loved was a squirt of Cabochard perfume from a black-and-white atomizer. I tilted my head for a spritz, and she obliged.

Phyllis would arrive, pull her coral Oldsmobile into the driveway, honk twice, and wait with the engine running. Her impatience seemed to steal my last few moments with Mom. Headlights shone into the living room when Mom opened the front door. Just across the room, my dad was watching TV. He liked *The Fugitive* or *Maverick*. Mom gave me a Camel cigarette-scented peck on the lips and was gone. Sometimes I called her at the Gardena Club before I went to bed. I knew the number by heart. I would ask the operator to page M. Sullivan and, after a couple minutes, she would come to the phone to say goodnight.

On Gardena nights, I helped my dad watch Mikey. First, I checked the kitchen and then swept through each room. More than once I found her in the bathroom sitting on the floor smiling and giggling, rummaging in the bottom cabinet. She would have happily stayed there all night, but when I asked, she'd get up and leave the room. I took my responsibility seriously and made rounds regularly. If all was quiet and I had finished my homework, I watched TV with Dad. I'd sit on the left arm of his green Naugahyde recliner that he'd pull close to our Hoffman TV. A small glass ashtray rested on the right arm. We watched Lakers games and the Harlem Globetrotters.

When I was eight, Mom and I saw the movie *The Miracle Worker*. There, up on the big screen, was a family like ours! Helen Keller was blind, made unintelligible sounds, and slung her food around. Her family couldn't contain her. Just like our family and Mikey. But, thanks to Annie Sullivan, she got better. She began to talk and stopped throwing tantrums. Right in that theater I made a decision that I was going to be our family's Annie Sullivan. I became hopeful that I could show that Mikey was more than trainable. I would show that she was teachable. I would teach Mikey to communicate. I would set her free. We would be like real sisters, and my parents would be so happy.

Right away I went to work. I taught myself finger spelling and set out, privately so I could surprise my parents, to teach Mikey to say the word "cup." I predicted that, just like in the movie, once she "got it" a whole torrent of words would follow. I decided that "cup" could be our breakthrough. I was sure that she linked the word with the object. I thought a short word would be easier to say. I sat next to her on the couch, placed a cup in one of her hands and finger spelled "cup" in her other hand while saying the word. I realized later that finger spelling wasn't necessary for Mikey because she could hear me, but I think she enjoyed it even if it didn't mean anything to her.

Over many hours and weeks, she was patient with me. She sat quietly, held the cup, listened, and rocked, but sadly, I was unsuccessful. We had no Helen Keller happy ending.

In the diagnostic lingo of the day, Mikey was considered, at best, trainable. She responded with a broad smile to praise when mastering a new task. She was toilet trained and could wipe, somewhat effectively, if handed a piece of toilet paper. She loved, loved, loved to flush the toilet; she was delighted each time she heard the whoosh. She listened for the tank to fill then flushed it again. Enough flushes brought a verbal response from one of us, "OK, Mikey, that's enough." She might get up and wander to another room, or she might giggle and flush again. If someone pulled socks over her toes, she could finish pulling them up. "Lift your arm" meant we were going to put a t-shirt or sweater on her, and she obliged. She knew which room was hers and that mine was off limits.

She understood a lot of words and sentences. If I said "ride" or "let's go," she headed for the front door, eager for her favorite adventure, a car ride. "Step up" or "step down" meant that a curb was imminent, and she responded accordingly.

We think Mikey could say three words. They were garbled, barely understandable, but we were pretty sure. They were words that represented things that made her happy: "Mom," "tea," and "go."

By the time I was nine, I was giving Mikey her nighttime medications. I crushed the Mellaril, an antipsychotic that was used as a tranquilizer, as finely as possible, and then mixed it in warm tea with lots of sugar. It didn't dissolve completely, and a film of bitter powder always sat on top.

I felt my success at getting Mikey to take her medication had been the result of patience and honesty. She trusted me. She did what I asked. She knew who I was. My ability made me a valuable member of the team and earned me praise and appreciation from my parents, too.

I'd call Mikey and she'd come and sit in her chair. "It's time for your medicine." She waited, rocking gently. The room had to be quiet. If she was distracted, she was more likely to jump up and leave. I'd move a kitchen chair in front of her by picking it up, avoiding the noise of dragging it across the floor. Hearing that I sat in front of her, she'd reach out and lightly touch me. "Here you go," I'd say, as I touched the spoon gently to her lips. On the first try, she'd allow only the minutest amount, enough to tell what it was, but I'd patiently go on. "Come on, Mikey. I know it tastes bad, but you have to take it. I have some strawberries for you when we're done." On the next try, she'd let in a little more. It could take ten minutes to get one teaspoon down, but the Dilantin, prescribed to prevent seizures, was easy; it was a thick orange liquid that didn't taste bad at all.

When we finished, I always gave her what I had promised, strawberries, or I fed her some ice cream on a spoon.

alone together

Sometimes I had a parent all to myself. I baked peanut butter cookies with Mom, and we decorated chocolate cakes with powdered sugar sifted through a paper doily, leaving a white lacey pattern on the dark cake. She taught me to read, and we went to the library together once a week. She strolled through the grown-up aisles while I looked in the children's section. She always checked out the maximum, ten books, while I took two or three. My love of reading began when I was very young, and I read well before I began kindergarten. My mother read stories and poems to me. I memorized the poems of Robert Louis Stevenson and recited them for her. I went on to read Nancy Drew. But soon my favorite grown-up book was Jack London's *Call of the Wild*, a harbinger of the love I would always feel for dogs.

I was nine when, on one of my special together-with-Mom days, Mom took me to the Santa Monica Civic Auditorium to see a closed-circuit Beatles concert. I wore the white imitation leather John Lennon hat that I had gotten for Christmas. I wanted to look grown up—no matching mother-daughter dresses like I had worn as a little girl. Most of the other girls were teenagers. They didn't come with a parent. Mom and I arrived early and sat in the balcony. The Beatles were larger than life on the screen, but the quality of the picture was not very good. It was just about impossible to hear them sing because we were all screaming. When I looked to my right, I saw that Mom was screaming, too. What a great mom! Of course, I didn't realize at the time that she probably wasn't enthralled with the Beatles like I was. Oh, she probably liked them OK, but she was screaming so that we could share the experience together and, in the dark, strangers wouldn't witness her abandon.

Mom was strong and capable. It didn't matter if what was happening was routine, unexpected, or a full-blown disaster. She did what needed to be done. She put one foot in front of the other. She didn't cry or yell, didn't seem flustered. She wasn't demonstrative, except with Mikey. With Mikey, she was soft and gentle, and Mikey sometimes relaxed into the comfort of her voice and touch. I wanted Mom to be affectionate with me, too. But I thought that I was too old and that because Mikey was like a baby, she needed it more.

I believe that some of those emotions Mom held inside fueled her strength—that letting out too much would deplete her. Sometimes frustration would burble to the surface as "goddamnsonofabitchtohell." She didn't say it to anybody in particular, just mumbled it under her breath, letting off a little steam. Sometimes she cranked up the volume with the emphasis on key syllables: "godDAMNsonofaBITCHtoHELL!" She had a wry sense of humor, too. Quick and intelligent, although I didn't fully appreciate its subtlety until I was older.

Another person may have run away or buckled under the weight of the challenges she faced. Mom was the strong one, the responsible one. She was the one in her family who took care of her mother when she was dying from burns, and her father when he was diagnosed with terminal brain cancer. She went back to Illinois when her brother was admitted to an institution because of alcoholic brain damage. When her sister Phyllis attempted suicide and was admitted to a psychiatric hospital, my three young cousins came to stay with us for a while. Mom's best friend in Illinois, June, was diagnosed with paranoid schizophrenia. June's illness and subsequent withdrawal left Mom no one to share her troubles with. I think she yearned for her mother during these difficult times.

Dad helped shoulder the weight of the tragedies, but my parents didn't share the kind of intimacy that would have made their burdens a little lighter. I was much too young to understand.

There was tragedy in Dad's family, too. When I was five, Dad's older brother Joe, the one he was closest to, died in a plane crash, along with his wife, two little girls, and seventy-eigh other passengers. Only my eight-year-old cousin Bobby survived. We kept a copy of *Time* magazine with a picture of Bobby on the cover in the bottom drawer in the hall with all the other pictures. I think there were discussions about who would raise Bobby, and it was decided he would stay with his mother's family.

Mom told me later that Dad loved being a father. He stopped drinking beer after Mikey was born. When we were babies, he did whatever was needed at home. He changed diapers, rocked Mikey for hours, fed her, and gave up his sleep so Mom could get some.

He was strong, too—did what needed to be done. But he was softer, more affectionate. He loved to tell funny stories. A certain tone in his voice alerted his audience that one was coming. The adults groaned, but I loved hearing the same tales over and over again.

One of my favorites was about a "rarie." A rarie is a rare and harmless beast that lived in the woods outside of a town. The rarie kept coming into town strewing trashcans and trash along the streets and sidewalks. The people in town had only caught a glimpse of him because he came at night when everyone was sleeping. Finally, after weeks of waiting and watching, a man captured the rarie. He was large, furry, quiet, and completely non-threatening. The townspeople met to discuss what to do with him. Finally, they agreed to put him in the back of a truck and release him in the countryside, far away. When they arrived at the place where he was to be released, they backed the truck up to a ledge. The rarie looked down and saw that he was going to be dropped down a pretty steep hill and said, "That's a long way to tip a rarie." I didn't know that there was an old song, "It's a Long Way to Tipperary," about a county in Ireland. I just thought it was a wonderful story and asked to hear it over and over.

Dad was proud of his Irish heritage. I think he associated it with the most fun-loving time of his youth. If I had been born one day later, on St. Patrick's Day, I would have been named Patricia. He would have had a pair of girls nicknamed "Pat and Mike." Fine Irish names. Top that off with the last name of Sullivan. His favorite color was green, so mine was green, too. I have a piece of faux blarney stone on my porch.

Dad taught me to ride a bicycle, built me a playhouse in our backyard, and took me to Dodgers games.

During Easter vacation in the third grade, he and I took a trip to Santa Catalina Island, just the two of us. It took about two hours to get there on the "Big White Steamship." Mom drove us to the port in San Pedro and, as I walked toward the ship holding my dad's hand, I turned to see her waving from the car. I picture my dad and I walking hand in hand up the gangplank, him tall and lanky, wearing his usual short-sleeved shirt and loose-fitting trousers. He looked like Gregory Peck to me. I was wearing a light cotton dress and sneakers.

The ship was huge. On the main level, there was a large room with long varnished wood benches bolted to the wood deck. Windows lined both sides of the room, allowing passengers to watch the sea during the trip. There was a snack/soda/cocktail bar at one end of the room, and the other end was open to the outside deck.

Once the trip got underway, after we had sandwiches and soda, young children were shuffled to another large room on the lower deck. There were no windows there, no need for a view, because we were there to be entertained by a clown. I've never been partial to clowns. Not because they're scary; they're just not the least bit entertaining. I would rather have been with my dad. I sat patiently with the other children watching as the clown, with his white face and orange tennis-ball nose, pranced about the stage, distracting the children so their parents could enjoy a childfree voyage upstairs. He made blue balloon dogs, pink balloon bunnies, and yellow balloon hats and walked through the audience as the children squealed to get one of his creations. I was not interested.

Once the clown act was over, thankfully, we re-joined our parents on the top deck. We had almost a half hour before we docked in Catalina, and Dad and I spent most of our time outside. It was sunny and warm. A brisk, salty breeze whipped my hair and left a cool mist on my skin. The ocean was deep blue, almost black, choppy and roiling, nothing like the tranquil beaches we had at home. Dad and I stood at the rail and watched large gray or white gulls circling behind the ship hooting and diving to the ocean surface. "Terry, look!" Dad was pointing at the ocean. I turned to see sparkling fish with wings flying alongside us, diving in and out of the water.

When we arrived at the Avalon Marina, suntanned young boys in cut-off shorts stood on the wooden dock. They called out to the passengers to throw coins. Dad handed me some to toss. The boys dove into the shallow clear water to retrieve them.

Our day was spent mostly walking up the main street that paralleled the marina and looking in all the five-and-dime tourist shops. I pulled Dad along, looking at tikis made of palm tree husks and abalone shell ashtrays. The trinkets were not any different from the ones in the tourist shops on the Santa Monica Pier.

There was one difference, however. Almost every store had grab bags. For ten cents, customers could reach in a barrel and grab a small brown paper bag. Each bag was tied with a colored ribbon—pink for girls, blue for boys, and yellow for either. I studied the bags before selecting one, trying to divine which had the best prize. Dad bought me a bracelet with little tiki heads on it. I still have it and keep it, with other mementos, in a small jewelry box.

There were saltwater taffy shops with machines in the window that stretched the rubbery pink candy. Dad bought roasted peanuts in the shell. We ate them from a brown paper bag as we walked. Later, we stopped to have hot dogs and pink lemonade. Years later, Dad chuckled when he told me that he bought the peanuts hoping to make me thirsty so we could sit down for a rest.

The sun, excitement, and all the walking tired both of us, and we were ready to go when the ship departed for the mainland late that afternoon. I know now how much he enjoyed remembering that day he spent with his little girl. I loved spending time with him, too.

princess

One day when I was nine, Mom, Mikey, and I picked Dad up from work, like we did on most weekdays, at 4:00 P.M. I held Mikey's hand down the porch steps and helped her get in the backseat of the car, so she didn't hit her head on the frame. Then I locked the latches and got in the front seat next to Mom. She turned on the radio to find some music with a strong bass beat. It was only about three miles to International Telemeter, where Dad worked as an electronic engineer developing a new technology—cable television.

We parked, and I walked inside the plain one-story brick building into a large room filled with drafting tables. It was a friendly place, and as I passed the men that Dad worked with, they said "Hi Terry" or "Here to get your dad?" I got to know many of their names because I visited often and Dad talked about them sometimes. Ron Mandel, Bill Rubenstein, and Mel Meyers.

Dad got behind the wheel, and I moved to the back seat with Mikey.

The West Los Angeles animal shelter was on the way home, and because Mikey was quiet I asked Mom, "Can we stop and see the dogs today?" I would have asked each day, but I knew not to push my luck. Some days it was obvious that we needed to get Mikey home. The close quarters of a car were less than ideal for a biting and hair-pulling incident. If Mikey was calm or only a little bit hyper, Dad could drive around for a few minutes so that I could go in to visit the shelter dogs. Mom and Dad glanced at each other, then she turned to me: "Okay, but just for a little bit."

Mom accompanied me inside. We entered through double glass doors. A woman behind the counter looked up, recognized me, and smiled and nodded as I headed toward the kennels. We entered a room filled with stacked cages, the cat and kitten room, though sometimes there were bunnies, too. We kept on going, through another swinging door, into the dog section. A long corridor stretched before us with ten runs on each side—boys on the right, girls on the left. Panels of fluorescent lights hung from the ceiling, but it was darker than the cat room, cool and damp. The kennel staff had just hosed down the concrete floors.

The first dogs that spotted us started barking and soon there was a cacophony as the others joined in. We were the only visitors. Mom waited quietly, standing near the door. She wasn't what you'd call a "dog person," but she knew dogs were special to me, and she indulged my desire to visit them. I hoped, but did not expect, that someday I would be able to bring one home.

I always visited the girls. I knew I didn't have much time, so I walked quickly down the corridor, all the way to the end, looking into each kennel. Then I started back up slowly. I was looking for the dog that I would visit that day. Several dogs were housed together in most kennels, and as I passed by many trotted toward the chain-link gate, barking, wagging, wiggling, and jumping up. Some were too small to compete with their cage mates for attention. Some were particularly shy and hesitant to come to the gate when I beckoned them. Some squeezed themselves into a corner at the back of the kennel, trembling.

A lot of people find the gregarious dogs most appealing, but I wanted to reach out to the reticent ones. I picked those that held back but looked at me as if to say, "See me. Please, see me." I was drawn to the most vulnerable and invisible ones. I felt protective and could relate to their feeling alone and invisible.

On most days, when I found my girl, I sat down on the concrete, cross-legged, as close to the gate as I could get and coaxed her to come forward. I waited patiently, speaking softly. Sometimes she approached me tentatively and licked the fingers I poked through the small openings in the gate, then turned and pressed the side of her body against the wires so I could pet her. I stroked her as well as I could within the constraints of the chain link. "Good girl," I cooed. Sometimes my chosen one wouldn't or couldn't come forward, and I would try again on my next visit if she were still there.

That day, as we were on our way out, we passed a baby pen in the cat room. I hadn't noticed it when we first came in. It was about four feet by four feet, with a mesh fabric on all sides and newspapers spread on the floor. Inside I saw a pair of little puppies, littermates I'm sure. They were mongrels, one gray and one black and white. I turned to Mom with a pleading look, "Aren't they cute? Can I hold one?"

Over the years, I'd had pets. When I was five, Mom brought home a tiny dachshund puppy with silky, reddish brown fur. She wiggled and covered my face with puppy-breath kisses when I cuddled her. I took her to kindergarten on "show and tell" day and planned to bring her back at the end of the school year so everyone could see how she had grown. We called her "Puppy," but I didn't have her long enough to give her a proper name. One evening, a few weeks later, Chucky, a playmate who lived a few houses away, was leaving our house to go home and didn't close the gate behind him. Puppy followed him across the street and was killed instantly when a car hit her. My parents put her little body in a cardboard box and placed it on the front porch for the city to pick up in the morning.

Dad acquiesced to my pleas, and I rode on his shoulders when he took me outside to see her. He carried me out to her at least three times before my bedtime. I peered at her still, little body. "Look, Daddy, I think she moved. Did you see?" I cried hopefully. That night when my father gave me my bath, Mom called out, "Don't forget to wash her face." He called back, "Every time I try, she starts crying again." I could feel his love and compassion. After that, I cried on purpose whenever he put the washcloth to my cheek, prolonging my bath and keeping him near until the water turned cold and I had to get out.

Puppy's accident was my first encounter with death. I asked God to take care of Puppy that night when I knelt beside my bed and said my bedtime prayers.

A couple of years later, one of my father's co-workers gave us a sweet Samoyed named Charlie. It was a thoughtful gift for a family with two young children. He was snowy white and fluffy with a big plumed tail, large black eyes, and a wet black nose. Charlie didn't stay very long either. One day, he approached Mikey, tail wagging, curious; maybe he wanted to play. After feeling his cold, wet nose, Mikey bit it. She was probably curious, too. A gentle dog, he cried out but never growled or snapped. My parents decided that he would be better off, safer, in a different home. I understood that Charlie had to leave. I hope he had a happy life.

A while after Charlie, we had a pair of large, beautiful white ducks. I named them Quacky and Wacky. They lived in the backyard, safe from Mikey, and romped in our little plastic wading pool. Sometimes, when Mikey and I were in the pool, Quacky and Wacky popped in and out of the water, flapping their wings. I splashed along with them while Mikey reclined on the side of the pool, enjoying the water, seemingly disinterested in what was happening around her.

And then one day Mom found Quacky dead. Apparently Wacky had pecked him to death. I know now that this isn't entirely uncommon. Alone now, Wacky never stopped quacking. He seemed horribly lonely without his companion, and Mom took him to the butcher and had him "dressed." When she served him for dinner, I couldn't eat him. I don't think Dad did either, but he never tried anything new. Mom grew up on a farm.

She was in the 4H club and favorite cows that she helped raise from birth were slaughtered for beef. She watched as her mother snapped the neck of a chicken then cooked him for dinner, so I don't think it crossed her mind that eating a duck that had been my pet would bother me. To this day I have never tasted duck, and I always think of Wacky when I see it on a menu.

Then there was Froggy. I guess I was about eight and spending a Saturday with my cousins, John and Jim. We often did kid stuff together, like making tents out of blankets that we threw over a clothesline and staked with rocks, then sneaking cigarettes and smoking until we were sick. That day, after we had been to a matinee, we crossed the street to a small park where we rolled down grass-covered hills and watched ducks and huge goldfish in a brackish pond.

We were peering into the pond and saw a big, fat, four-inch-long tadpole. I leaned over to catch him, slipped on a slope covered with slimy green algae, and slid into the water. I was wet, with a huge green stain on my yellow pants, but I had him in my hand. I put him in a fishbowl in my room at home to watch him turn into a frog.

One afternoon, a few weeks later, I crossed my room to feed Froggy and discovered that the fish bowl was empty. I was used to losses, but my belongings were usually safe if I kept them in my room. I began to look around and found pieces of tadpole scattered around the room—a leg on the dresser top, unrecognizable, stringy pieces lying on the floor. I like to think that Mikey was on a fishing expedition, for if she had been on a rampage, I'm sure I would have seen more damage. She had sneaked into the forbidden room and discovered the squishy delight. It was, I like to think, a merciful death for Froggy, a fate better than being confined to a small bowl, never to swim again with his friends in the big pond.

And now, nine years old and at the animal shelter, I stood next to the baby pen and hoped that Mom would let me hold a puppy. Bringing one home was risky. Mikey could easily severely injure or even kill her. And Mikey's safety was also a factor. The puppy might bite her if it was afraid. Mom probably didn't want to deny me some-thing of my own to love, something that would love me in return.

Mom nodded and said I could hold one of the puppies, "but only for a minute." I was too short to reach into the pen, so she put the black-and-white puppy in my arms. It was a girl. I stood still, holding her close to my chest. After a couple of minutes, Mom said, "It's time to go." I kissed the puppy goodbye and held her out to Mom to return to the pen. "No, I think we should bring her home. What do you think?" Did I hear her right? "Yes!" I held the puppy tighter as we went to the counter in the office so Mom could do the necessary paperwork.

When we returned to the car, I got into the front seat with Dad. "What have you got there?" he smiled.

"A puppy!"

I'm sure they had discussed the decision to bring another animal into our home. I was a responsible little girl, willing and able care for the puppy, and, apparently, deserving of such a precious gift. I named her Princess and, when I wasn't helping my parents with Mikey, she was my companion and playmate, a sweet part of the respite I found in my room.

fourth grade

In the fourth grade, Anne and I were inseparable. Graduating from Beatles to boys, we became enamored of two sixth-graders. David, Anne's interest, was slender with always-tousled blond hair and fine features. Allen had auburn hair and was more gregarious. We were convinced that if we could join the sixth-grade clique of cool kids, David and Allen might want us as girlfriends. The most popular girls wore nylons and makeup. They smoked and looked very sophisticated. One morning, I snuck some suntan-colored nylons and garters from my mom's bureau drawer and put them on in the girls' bathroom at school, along with a little lipstick. The sixth graders had a laugh at my orangish-colored legs. They weren't cruel but made it clear that I was too young to be considered one of them.

Most mornings, before leaving for school, I took quarters from a lunch-money jar. The first day that Allen asked me for a quarter, I swooned at the attention and gladly gave it to him. He asked the next day again. "Can I have another one?" "Thaaaank you. You're so wonderful." Taking more quarters from the jar, I gave some to Anne so she could entice David. By dispensing them one at a time, we prolonged the delicious attention. After a couple of weeks, a teacher observed our antics, and she sent me to Principal Schwartz's office. Anne didn't have to go.

Principal Schwartz wasn't very tall. He had dark hair, a swarthy complexion, and wore heavy glasses. I had seen him walking into the school offices and at school assemblies, but he had never spoken to me. I had never seen him smile, and he didn't smile that day when I sat across from him.

"I've been informed by your teacher that you and Anne Nelson have been giving money to some of the sixth-graders. I assume that your parents are unaware of this?" He looked directly at me.

I looked away. "Yes."

"This must stop immediately. I will be calling your mother when our meeting is over."

Oh no, I clenched the chair arms.

I knew that my behavior would embarrass Mom.

"I've instructed teachers that you are not to spend time with or speak with Anne."

I think I understood, even then, that the teachers thought my alliance with Anne could lead to trouble ahead. Banishment from my friendship with her seemed like a severe punishment for my infraction, but I didn't say anything, other than "Okay." I had never been reprimanded before and wouldn't dream of challenging an authority figure.

"You can return to your class now."

When I came home from school that day, Mom told me that the school had called her. She didn't say it outright, but I knew that she was disappointed in me. I knew because she made that particular movement with her mouth that looked as though she had peanut butter stuck to the roof. It meant she was exasperated. I think she was more troubled that I had taken the quarters than that I had given them away. It was inconsiderate of me to make trouble, to draw attention to myself in a negative way. It was crushing to think that she thought I was bad. She would tell my dad, and he would be disappointed, too. But his disappointment would be about my behavior, not about my character. I vowed to myself that I wouldn't cause trouble again. I was lucky my parents didn't ban my friendship with Anne.

When the quarters stopped, the attention from David and Allen stopped, too. It wasn't the last time I would yearn for the attention and affection of a man who didn't care for me.

The prohibition from speaking to each other at school seemed ridiculous to Anne and me. It bolstered our union. It was now "them" and "us," and we looked for creative ways to circumvent our sentence. In our classroom, seats were arranged in a horseshoe. Our teacher moved about within the U, occasionally turning her back to write on the blackboard. Anne and I sat opposite each other. I had finally found a practical application for finger spelling, and I taught Anne. We didn't have to look at each other to communicate. With a hand resting casually on the desk, one of us spelled with hardly noticeable movement while facing the front of the class. The other wrote down the letters until the message was complete. Then we switched. We were wildly successful, not speaking to each other throughout the class.

An event that shook the country happened while I was in the fourth grade. On November 22, 1963, I was nine years old. It was recess when, unexpectedly, the alarm rang, signaling that recess was over. As we returned to our classes, a cluster of teachers met us and directed us to the auditorium. Teachers were circulating in the room as it filled with students. Some of them were crying. The principal announced that President Kennedy had been assassinated and that our parents had been contacted to pick us up. Soon the street in front of the school was filled with cars, our moms dropping everything to take us home.

My mother drove up in our station wagon. She held a crumpled tissue, catching tears that streamed down her flushed face. It was the first time I saw my mother cry.

slam

By the time Mikey was eleven, she had more bad days than good. She was stronger and more violent. As always, my parents looked for possible causes for her outbursts, or explosions, as we called them. Mom said it was as if a pilot light went off in her head. People refer to the outbursts of children with autism as tantrums, yet, to me, tantrum implies volition. Often, I think her outbursts were far beyond her control.

I did my best to defend myself from Mikey's attacks, the biting, scratching, and hair pulling. I pushed her away, pulled her hair, or grabbed her arm. Sometimes I had to hit her, but I wasn't retaliating, only protecting myself. Sometimes I just avoided her, staying in my room.

As I headed to my bedroom one afternoon, I passed her in the hall. I wanted to go by unnoticed, so I was careful to be quiet. The hall was wide. I had plenty of room to avoid her, but she heard me.

Immediately, she tore into her wrist, biting deeply. The scarred flesh was barely healed from recent attacks. Her face contorted, and she made fierce, unintelligible sounds, muffled by a mouthful of flesh. She reached out with her free arm and nearly

found me, but I jumped away, and then rushed forward to intervene, to try to pull her teeth away from her wrist without tearing
her flesh further. She turned her attack on me, grabbing my arm
and biting down hard. "No," I yelled and grabbed a fistful of
her hair, close to the scalp for greater leverage. I tried to pull her
mouth away before she broke the skin. I had had years of practice
managing these events. We were about the same size, neither tall
nor short, and slender bordering on skinny. But at that moment,
she was stronger. She gripped me powerfully with her teeth, but
my determination matched hers, and as I continued to pull, she
let go. Luckily, I escaped with only a bite impression on my arm
that would disappear.

Mikey turned and stormed into her bedroom, which was
only a few feet away. The door slammed into the wall, and the
doorknob smashed through the fresh plaster that had been opti-
mistically applied by my dad over an older puncture. She crossed
the room and threw herself onto the twin bed that was pushed
against the wall. Moaning and writhing, lying on her back, her
bare feet pummeled the wall until the plaster gave way, leaving a
gaping black hole. Finally spent, she crumpled. Curled up, facing
the wall, she whimpered. This explosion was passing. Mom had
come from the kitchen and approached quietly. We stood silently
together at the door, watching for a moment to make sure it was
over. There was nothing more to do, nothing to say, so Mom
gently pulled the bedroom door almost closed—leaving enough
room to peek in to check on her.

It was quiet, but the interlude was fragile. Any noise, a door
closing, voices too loud, a toilet flushing, could end the precious
peace and precipitate Mikey's bolting out of bed and her fierce
self-mutilation. We slunk to our personal space, Mom back to the
kitchen to prepare dinner, and me to my room just down the hall.
If we were lucky, our respite would last a couple of hours.

As she got stronger, car rides became risky, too. One day
Mom and Dad took Mikey for a drive, hoping to calm her down
during an outburst. Slowly and quietly, Dad circled the city over

and over. It was too dangerous in the back, so Mom sat up front with him. Her voice was the only one that might calm Mikey, so when Mikey continued to bite herself, Mom spoke softly to her. But this time, it only seemed to increase the power of the outburst. The ride wasn't working. They started home. Maybe the outburst would dissipate if Mikey had more room to flail. But they didn't get back in time. Mikey had begun to kick at the car doors and windows. Just as they pulled into our driveway, she broke the glass. Fortunately, she was uninjured.

Shortly after that, we went to see the new unit for blind and mentally retarded girls at Fairview State Hospital. The grounds resembled a small town, with a main road that wound for miles around the perimeter. Narrow adjoining streets led to cul-de-sacs, each with four barrack-like wards.

Entering Unit 27, the blind girls' ward, was eerie. We faced a long white corridor with white walls and spotless white linoleum floors. Brilliant fluorescent ceiling lights exaggerated the brightness. About fifteen girls, most about Mikey's age, were sitting in plastic chairs lined up against the corridor walls. The girls were all dressed but looked a bit disheveled—wrinkled clothing, mismatched shoes. Some sat on their haunches; several were rocking. One or two fidgeted with their hands. Most were silent, but some made sounds like Mikey did. A couple of the girls reached their arms out when they heard our footsteps, as if to say, "Are you here for me?" We walked down the corridor in silence.

A nurse took us on a brief tour. I think my parents had already decided this place wasn't good enough for Mikey. We were quiet when we returned to our car. My parents didn't say what they thought about Unit 27. I don't think they expected it to be perfect, but they must have hoped it would be acceptable—hoped that it could help both them and Mikey. Mikey would not be refused admission here, but she deserved better than warehousing.

mom & dad

Once Mom started going out to play poker, she never came home before I went to bed. When I got up in the morning, she was sleeping on a twin bed in her room. Mikey and I each had a room at opposite ends of the hall. Dad slept in Mikey's room. I don't remember a time when my parents shared a bedroom.

I was often the first one up in the mornings. The house would be quiet as I got ready for school. I'd go into Mom's room to get quarters for lunch from a cup she kept on her dresser. As I passed her bed, I could see the pan that she kept pushed underneath. She woke during the night to retch into it. Many years later, she told me that she thought she threw up because she "just couldn't stomach it anymore." I'm not sure what she meant by "it" – maybe the whole situation, maybe her marriage. When she told my Dad how she felt, he said, "If I can take it, so can you."

I'd pause to watch Mom sleeping. Her face was etched with fatigue. She wore a fine mesh hairnet that covered pink foam hair rollers. A stained, heavy, half-filled mug of yesterday's tea, with the Lipton string hanging over the side, sat on the bedside table next to an ashtray full of cigarette butts. Mom drank her tea black—dark black because she never removed the bag—with lots of sugar. One cup sometimes lasted all day. She took a sip when she had a chance. It didn't seem to matter that it got cold.

There were always seven or eight library books stacked on the floor by her bed, and I think now that Mom must have found fiction a better escape than sleep, though the price she paid was exhaustion.

Dad slept on a mattress on the floor, set in front of the door of Mikey's room. If she woke and tried to leave, he would be able to avert a disaster. Although we whispered, didn't flush the toilet, and kept the TV low after 9:00 P.M. while we waited for Mikey to fall asleep, she was often awake all night—sometimes screaming, sometimes giggling, so Dad didn't get much sleep either.

It was on nights when Mom was out, Mikey was crying, and Dad was trying to quiet her that I would have strange dreams. I wouldn't call them nightmares, but I was troubled during the dreams and relieved to wake up. In each one, I was surrounded by darkness. I felt like I was underwater but not drowning. I heard muffled sounds coming from a distance, like a record played at the slowest speed. Were they voices? I reached out into the darkness searching for a wall or a person—something to touch, to get my bearings. But there wasn't anything there. I tried to speak, but my voice was soft and I knew no one could hear me—if there was, in fact, anyone there at all. I felt alone and powerless. I wondered if Mikey's world was like my dreams.

At about the same time, Dad's job changed and he started traveling out of state. He was gone for several days at a time and Mom was alone, caring for Mikey twenty-four hours a day. I helped as much as I could, but I was still a child. When I was at school, Mom had no one to help her.

Looking back, I believe that my parents' marriage, by this time, continued only because of Mikey. There was no escape. Each lived for his or her brief respite—my mother for her nights out and my father for work. Coming home, for either of them, became increasingly difficult. No sleep, no marriage, no help, no hope.

commitment

When Mikey was twelve, she was strong enough to pull Mom or me out the front door when she wanted to go for a ride. Her episodes of self-mutilation and destruction became more severe and more frequent. The days of watching her twirl to Chipmunks songs were a distant memory. She was agitated, biting and throwing things, banging her head. Dad stopped patching the wall plaster that she kicked out. Sometimes it took two people to restrain her. She only slept for brief periods in spite of the Phenobarbital we gave her. Her cries were mournful and despairing. Doctors tried new medications called "major tranquilizers"— Thorazine and Stelazine. If it ended in "-zine," it made her worse. The doctors didn't listen to my parents; maybe they just didn't know of anything else to try.

Mikey sometimes had an agonized expression as she rubbed her eyes and pushed them in, crying. Her head banging seemed worse at these times. When the sun shone on her suddenly, like during a ride in the car, she cried out and bit herself. My parents considered having her eyes removed in hopes of alleviating what seemed to be searing pain, but doctors said her eyes couldn't cause her pain and that, because of adhesions, they could not react to light. Again, Mom and Dad's observations and understanding of Mikey's feelings and behavior were out of sync with what the doctors believed. But my parents were with Mikey constantly and loved her; nobody knew her better than we did.

Mom worried that if her eyes were removed, Mikey would surely take the artificial eyes out. Most people already avoided her and with her eyes removed they would be even more repulsed by her appearance. Driving them further away might deprive Mikey of any kindness from strangers, a kindness that she might someday have to rely upon. So she kept her eyes. Much later we learned that the only boy we knew who was even a little bit like Mikey, Johnny, had had his eyes removed for similar reasons. He was able to tell his parents that he didn't know how much pain he had suffered all his life until it went away.

Always, unanswered questions hovered. Is it possible that Mikey understands everything but is trapped in a body that can't communicate? Is it possible that only the part of her brain that controls communication is damaged and that intolerable frustration drives her behavior? If only we could break through, would she be able to participate fully in life? Her suffering was heartbreaking for all of us.

I still struggle when I hear stories about non-verbal children or adults who have breakthroughs, the ones who find a way to belong to the world because of a computer or talented teachers. Everything changes for them. They have a future, and their families have hope. I want to be happy for them. They must be joyous. But I often turn the television off when such stories appear. I resent them and am ashamed of my feelings. I find little comfort by telling myself that their chances must have been better because they were higher-functioning than Mikey.

On Friday night, October 29, 1965, Mom and I were home with Mikey. My dad was en route from Shreveport, Louisiana where he'd supervised the rollout of a cable television system. Normally Mom, Mikey, and I would pile into the station wagon a half-hour before his plane was due and leave to pick him up. It was usually pretty late, 10:00 or 11:00 P.M., and we often went to Arlene's Donut Shop on the way home.

When I came back from school that afternoon, Mom said it had been a rough day. By early evening Mikey was wild, a tornado of destruction twirling violently, flailing her arms, biting, making indescribable noises. If one of us was able to pull her wrist away from her mouth, she just twisted her head and bit into her upper arm. If we'd had a medication that would help calm her, there was no way to force it into her. If Dad had been there, he might have been able to contain her, but it was too much for Mom and me. We moved things out of her way, tried to talk her down, and waited for her to exhaust herself. Surely this couldn't go on indefinitely. Mom, Dad, and I functioned on autopilot at times like this. Safety was our primary concern. Whatever I may have felt was buried beneath the adrenalin, the need to be totally focused, to keep Mikey, my parents, and myself from harm—as much as was possible.

Mikey raged into the kitchen. A large curtainless window next to the table was black with night, a stark contrast to the brightly lit yellow walls. She stumbled into the table and chairs as she continued lashing out. The obstacles only seemed to enrage her more. We followed her in, watching and waiting for an opportunity to intervene.

"Terry!" Mom said. "Go get a sheet, a flat sheet. Hurry."

I ran to the hall, grabbed a sheet from the linen cabinet and rushed back. Mom handed me one end of the sheet. "Hold it tight," she said. "We're going to try to wrap her up."

We positioned ourselves behind Mikey, one on each side with the sheet extended to enclose her. It was tight quarters. It would be difficult for her to escape before we could get her wrapped in our makeshift straitjacket. I don't think Mom had a plan beyond containment, but at least we could stop her from hurting herself further. Maybe she would calm down.

Mom signaled me, and we both moved forward quickly to cross in front of Mikey and wrap her tightly. But we couldn't get her arms at her sides. We tried again and failed.

Suddenly, Mikey paused. She must have been exhausted. Maybe a sound or a thought distracted her. Mom said, "Mikey, do you want to go for a ride?" She held still for a moment and then bolted for the front door. Mom followed behind her, calling out, "Get my purse."

It was dangerous to try a car ride, but we hoped it would calm her down long enough to drive to the County Hospital emergency room. I sat in the back seat with Mikey, as far away from her as I could get but ready to intervene if she grabbed for Mom's hair. We hoped she wouldn't kick a window out.

The emergency room was bright. Two strong-looking men took Mikey. I stood alone while Mom spoke with hospital staff. Then there was paperwork to complete. "They're keeping her here," Mom said as we walked to the car. The doctors would evaluate Mikey.

It was late. The entire trip to the hospital had taken about three hours. Dad was home when we walked in the front door. He had waited for us at the airport, and, when we didn't arrive, had taken a cab home. I had never seen him look afraid, as he did then. Mom quickly said, "We're okay. We're okay. We had to take Mikey to County." His body visibly relaxed, and the look of panic changed to a questioning one. We all sat in the kitchen as Mom calmly told him what had happened. When she finished, I witnessed a moment of tenderness that I had never seen them share. A door to the unknown had been opened that night. I believe now that they relinquished some of the hope that they had clung to for so many years. Without speaking or touching, they acknowledged each other's breaking heart.

By now it was almost morning. It didn't seem likely that anyone could go to sleep, so we went to Arlene's donut shop, just as we had on so many other nights, and ate donuts together in the car.

Mom and Dad received a subpoena to appear at County Hospital's court on Tuesday, November 2. I went with them to the hearing.

The courtroom looked just like those on *Perry Mason*. The walls and furniture were wooden. Rows of chairs faced the front of the room, and a rail separated the spectators from clerks and sheriff's deputies. The judge, wearing a black robe, sat above everyone else, facing us. A uniformed guard brought Mikey into the room strapped in a wheelchair. As he handed her over to a different guard, he said, "Be careful. She bites." I don't know if my parents were given the option of taking Mikey home, or if the decision to commit her was made entirely by the judge based on input from the doctors. Ten minutes after Mikey was brought in, she was declared a ward of the court and committed to Camarillo State Hospital. My parents were no longer her guardians.

She left for Camarillo State Hospital immediately after the hearing. I stood next to my parents in the parking lot as we watched someone lead Mikey up the steps into a long, black-and-white Los Angeles County Sheriff's bus. It was hard to see the inside of the bus because there were bars on the windows, but as the bus pulled away, we could see Mikey near the center, sitting by the window, rocking. That day, the foundation of my world began to crack.

part two

Intersections

camarillo

We were required to wait for three days before we could visit Mikey. Dad took the day off from work and I stayed home from school. It was warm and sunny when we set out. We took the scenic coastal route, a longer drive than the freeway. The sun sparkled on the dark blue ocean and the waves crashed against the rocky shore, which became more rugged as we drove north. It seemed as though by choosing the leisurely, pretty route as opposed to the faster, stark freeway, we were trying to inject some optimism into our trip. After we had driven for nearly an hour, the road became a series of tight twists and sharp turns as we neared the hospital.

Camarillo State Hospital looked sleepy and peaceful as we drove onto the grounds. Acres of green rolling lawns were dappled with shade from ancient oak trees. Old Spanish Mission–style buildings with white arched doorways and red tile roofs were scattered throughout the property. A couple of patients—or maybe they were staff—strolled leisurely on meandering pathways.

We followed signs and drove a quarter of a mile down the main road to a large two-story administration building, more Spanish architecture with dark wood and colorful tiles inside. We were given directions to the adolescent girls' unit where Mikey was quartered. It was a short drive away. We rang the bell next to the barred door. A pudgy middle-aged woman with a pasty complexion, a rumpled ill-fitting dress, and a jangling mass of keys let us in.

A barrage of teenage girls immediately swarmed us: "Do you have a cigarette?" "Please, could I have a cigarette?" My parents scrambled to find Camels and smiled kindly at each girl as they handed her a cigarette, hoping, I'm sure, that their generosity would engender a bit of kindness toward Mikey.

The attendant shooed the girls away, and we stood looking into a large room—the "day room." Sunlight shone through mesh-covered windows high on the walls. There were comfortable-looking padded green vinyl chairs with chrome arms and a couple of matching couches. To the right was an office that had a view of the day room. Two staff women seemed busy and ignored us. To the left, a hallway led to unseen rooms. We spotted Mikey rocking in a chair. She jumped up as soon as she heard my parents speaking with the attendant, having recognized their voices immediately. Still unfamiliar with the layout of the room, she stumbled into a chair on her way to find us. Her face lit up when her outstretched hand reached my mother. It was like she was saying, "Thank God you found me. Let's get out of here. I want to go home."

We followed the attendant as she shuffled down a wide corridor toward an empty room where we could visit. Mom and Dad each held one of Mikey's hands, and she rocked happily between them. I trailed behind. It was a quiet visit. Mom brushed Mikey's hair, cooing and praising her. She seemed to enjoy the treats we brought—animal crackers, mints, and juice. An hour later, when it was time to leave, Mikey clung to my mom—desperately. "We'll come back, Mikey," Mom said, encouraging her to let go. "You have to stay here for now. You're such a good girl." Finally, the attendant pulled Mikey away, not gently. She held a finger to her lips, telling us to be quiet so Mikey wouldn't know we were still there. She pointed to the door and then locked it behind us.

When the next Saturday arrived, we set out for Camarillo again. This time, we were bringing Mikey home for an overnight visit. Mom brought some clothing for Mikey, everything marked in permanent black ink with her name and unit number. Each item was logged in, and Mom got a copy of the form. After a few minutes, Mikey was brought out to us. Dad signed a log noting the time we left the unit and the time we expected to return. When the attendant unlocked the door, Mikey forged ahead, pulling my parents along. She was oblivious to any steps or hazards ahead of her, and my parents had to slow her down before she tumbled down the concrete steps. I tagged along behind. She was happy and stayed happy all the way home. Mom had brought some cold cuts and cantaloupe and Mikey gobbled them up.

Her first visit home went well. Her spinning was happy and relaxed, and there was no biting. She got to have her favorite foods and soak in a long bath.

Mom inspected her body. There were some bruises, probably from bumping into obstacles in her new and unfamiliar environment. Mikey was the only blind patient, so it was unlikely that staff or patients took care to push chairs under tables or leave doors all the way open. Her left wrist still had raw areas over old scars. It looked like there were fresh bite marks, too.

When we took her back the next day, girls asking for cigarettes accosted us again, so my parents gave each one a cigarette and they rushed off. Mikey clung to Mom. She didn't want to let go, as though she was saying, "Wait a minute. I thought you got this all straightened out. This is all wrong. Don't leave me here." The attendant pulled Mikey away and said to us, "It's better if you don't prolong this. Just go. She'll be okay." So we went home, back to our new life without Mikey.

Our routines didn't change abruptly. Dad went to work, I went to school, and Mom began to go out a little earlier.

Occasionally, in the evenings, Dad and I drove a few blocks to Jan and Joe's liquor store. The man behind the counter knew us and would say, with a smile and wink, "What can I get for you?" Dad would say, "A Snickers bar for me." Then, looking down at me, his hand on my shoulder, he'd add, "and she'll have a six pack of Miller." The man went along with our little joke.

But everything was different at home. The rooms felt larger. The house was quiet. There was no need to retreat to my bedroom to find refuge.

There were no children's songs playing, no food to cut up, no messes to clean, and no medications to give. No one made regular rounds to see where Mikey was, and there was no need to go for aimless car rides. The garage door was unlocked. Dad put his mattress on a box spring, although my parents continued to sleep in different rooms. We could have the proverbial dinnertime gathering to share the events of the day without worrying about upsetting Mikey too much. But we were accustomed to refraining. Maybe we didn't have much to say.

Mikey and I had our own kind of connection, but our relationship wasn't one of affection and confidences. I hadn't lost a playmate or a friend, but I felt lonely.

My grades began to drop. Bs turned to Cs. The checkmarks for class participation on my report card went from high to low. Miss Mitchell, my sixth-grade teacher, wrote a note three months after Mikey was committed: "Teresa has turned in very little work this past quarter. I understand that often she is not able to do her homework. I've asked her to turn it in when able, but Teresa has not done this." I didn't know about the report card until decades later, when I discovered it in my mother's belongings, along with Girl Scout badges and other mementos of my childhood.

Mikey's vulnerability and the magnitude of her needs had given us purpose. She had been the main link in a chain that held us all together.

It may have been inevitable that Mikey was institutionalized. My parents had kept her at home longer than many parents would have. We never discussed it, but I think we knew that she would never live with us again.

winding road

We continued to bring Mikey home for weekend visits. We saw marks on her left wrist, and knew that she was biting herself. When we brought her back to her unit, my parents asked about it and the attendants told them that she was a problem and had grabbed and bitten other patients.

The first burn we found was on the soft underside of Mikey's forearm. It was an ugly blister, the size and shape of a lit cigarette. Mom and Dad brought it to the attention of the staff member who let us in one Sunday when we returned Mikey to the unit. They were assured that it must have been accidental. The nurse would be notified.

During Mikey's first year at Camarillo, each visit brought new horrors.

The doctors started her on Thorazine. My parents tried to explain that it only made her worse, but the doctors didn't listen. After all, these new drugs worked wonders on people with schizophrenia, sedating them into shuffling zombies and making life easier for the staff. My parents could share their experience and provide the doctors with information, but they had no control over what drugs the doctors ordered. They probably thought my parents were a nuisance.

I'm certain that the attendants didn't crush Mikey's pills. Surely they didn't use sweetened tea to coax her to take her medicine and then praise her when she complied like we did at home. When Mikey was agitated and the staff, determined to sedate her, couldn't force a pill down her throat, they gave her a shot. On visits home, Mom always examined Mikey's body when she was in the bathtub. She found swollen areas on her hips and reddened spots on her buttocks from the injections. One time, as Mikey sat in the tub, Mom saw that an injection site on her buttocks had become infected. There was a hole the size of a dime, about a quarter inch deep, filled with pus.

It didn't take Mikey long to learn that when we were in the car, and she felt the highway begin to wind, she was being taken back to Camarillo. She would begin to flail, bite herself, and reach out to grab whoever was near. There was no consoling her. After a while, we stopped using the winding coastal route and traveled on the straight freeway. It took less time. It was better to get the trip over with.

Back at her unit, Mikey clung tightly to Mom when the attendants pulled her away. We had told the staff that we called her Mikey, but they always called her Michele. When Mikey didn't respond, not realizing that she was being spoken to, it probably made them angry.

Mikey was nothing like the other girls on her unit. The only thing they had in common was their age. The other girls were seriously troubled delinquents whose parents couldn't manage them at home. They could all speak and see, and had no cognitive deficits. They may have been a danger to themselves and others, but not for the same reasons that Mikey was. Mikey was an aberration to them.

Rarely did we see Mikey without cigarette burns, a fat lip, or a black eye. When my parents would ask an attendant about the injuries, they would receive answers along the lines of, "Well, I dunno, I guess she does it to herself." Several times, when we arrived to visit, the attendant didn't know where Mikey was, and with irritation, would leave her jigsaw puzzle or put down her knitting to go find her. I had forgotten one incident until I encountered a paper I had written many years later:

On one such occasion, we looked down the hall to see a patient grab hold of Mikey's head and slam it into a wall. The attendant severely reprimanded Mikey for making so much noise when she cried.

My parents' cautious complaints were answered only with irritation. They were told they were over-protective.

When we arrived one day to pick Mikey up, the other girls clustered around us, as they always did, asking for cigarettes. There were four or five of them. My parents were always nice to the girls—Mikey was at their mercy. "I help give Mikey a bath," one of them said, hoping to earn a cigarette. "And I help dress her," another chimed in. "I help feed her." My parents smiled, passing out the smokes. Then one girl spoke up earnestly, "I'm not gonna burn her anymore." Mikey was the perfect victim. She couldn't see them coming, she couldn't defend herself, and she couldn't tell anyone what they were doing to her.

I wish that my parents had told me what they were doing to help Mikey. I wish they had told me that they were stomping their feet, rattling cages, going over heads, and demanding that Mikey be protected. I was eleven when Mikey was institutionalized. Maybe they thought they were doing the right thing by not involving me. "Let her be a little girl. She doesn't need to worry about this." I know that they were afraid to rock the boat, to make waves. They were afraid that Mikey would bear the brunt of an angry staff member and be punished. I stood by and observed, trying to be helpful where I could. We each suffered our feelings alone. I can only assume my parents, in their fractured marriage, felt the same emotions I felt—powerlessness, loneliness, anger, and guilt. I was a child, but I was also like a miniature parent. Even now, in spite of the distance of decades and the wisdom and perspective of experience, I cannot, in my heart, separate myself from our shared responsibility for her suffering.

I understood later that the barriers to getting Mikey out of that unit were steep. There were rules against housing adolescents on adult units. The state hospital system was mired in red tape, incompetence, and apathy.

dear diary

Back in the normal world, I began junior high. Mom and Dad gave me my first diary when I was in the seventh grade. The cover was a red, green, and white plaid fabric, and it locked with a tiny key. The introduction said: "There are no more precious possessions than memories; no greater pleasure than the remembrance of past happiness. A diary is a friend to go through life with, sharing your thoughts and experiences—remembering them for you." I kept many journals over the years. I kept them in a blue plastic portable file box and hauled them around, from place to place, for decades. But, once I put them away, I seldom glanced at them again. Until I began the story I am telling here.

I wrote about Mikey's visits home but didn't record the details.

JANUARY 3 - Tue.

Dear Diary,
School was ok today
It was like usual. Mom And
Dad took mikey back, she
was real unhappy about going
back. I don't seem to cry
about her as much. I wasn't
very friendly with her And
now I feel guilty about it.
I really love her.
(I Didn't go)

I was touched when I rediscovered this entry. Touched by my tender feelings toward Mikey. I never told anyone that I loved her.

I wrote about the normal side of my life: sleepovers, homework, what I wore to school, pimples, and boys.

JANUARY 4, 1966: I don't understand why boys don't like me. I'm getting worried about it. My New Year's resolution is to try to get in better shape and get boys to take a little interest in me. I'll probably need all the luck I can get!

I made an apron in my homemaking class, played cello in the orchestra, and went to slumber parties at girlfriends' homes. We went to chaperoned dances on Friday nights. The boys clustered on the opposite side of the dim room, and I hoped the one I liked would ask me to dance to a slow song, like Smokey Robinson's "Tracks of My Tears."

Anne and I were in the same Girl Scout troop and part of a

larger circle of girls where loyalties were fluid. Best friends became second-best friends and back again. I turned thirteen that year.

The school sent my parents a letter:

Dear Parent or Guardian,

Your daughter, Teresa Sullivan has been selected to participate in an excelled instructional program for academically talented seventh grade pupils which will begin with the spring semester. The program is designed to provide enriched experiences and excelled programs of study for these pupils so that they may have academic challenges which will help them to more fully develop their talents and learning capacity.

In evaluating last year's program it was found that students who participated had an increased interest in school subjects—were more aware of— curious about—and had a better understanding of their environment. In addition new and stimulating friendships are made.

I suppose the invitation was based on standardized testing done in the sixth grade.

It seems that my declining grades and participation in class had been overlooked when I transitioned from elementary to junior high school. While I may have had the intellectual ability to excel, I doubt that instability at home, stressors, and coping skills were considered.

JANUARY 4: I'm scared about going into XL classes but proud too.

Mom often prepared a simple roast before she left for the card club. On most afternoons, when I came home from school, she gave me cooking instructions so that I could have dinner ready when my dad came home. While the roast was cooking, I fixed Pillsbury biscuits, the kind from a cardboard tube that I rapped on the edge of the kitchen counter to open, and Jolly Green Giant green beans. Dad seemed to particularly appreciate that I put his glass in the freezer for a few minutes because he liked his milk really cold. We ate together, and after I had washed the dishes, we watched TV or I went to my room.

When Dad was out of town on a business trip and Mom was out all night, I sometimes stayed overnight at my friend Sharlon's house. Her big brother had had polio when he was younger and was in a wheelchair. We shared the invisible bond of coming from a family that was different, although mine was more extreme. We played Monopoly and told ghost stories. I worried about Princess, my steadfast companion, home alone all night. Sharlon, regretfully, was one of the friends that I left behind as I chose to spend time with more rebellious kids, including Anne. Sometimes I stayed home alone when my parents were both gone. It seems strange now that I was unsupervised all night at thirteen, but I didn't think anything about it at the time.

Another diary entry chronicles the time Anne and I tried to shoplift some makeup from a local market and were caught by the manager.

> *FEBRUARY 20: The manager called Mom, and I went home on the bus. Mom had a long talk with me. She said maybe I need a psychiatrist. I don't really mind being caught, but I feel like crying every time I think of what my mother thinks of me.*

She was probably right about the psychiatrist, but at that time I perceived the comment to mean that I was bad, rather than that I needed help. I think she looked at it that way, too. Being a problem was bad and selfish. Looking back, it would have been good to have some psychological support. Perhaps it could have helped all of us cope with the trauma of Mikey's circumstances.

Maybe we could have shared our feelings and I wouldn't have felt so alone. But, in our family, there was an unspoken understanding that it was important to maintain control of one's emotions in order to attend to the task at hand.

> *APRIL 11: I got an Unsatisfactory in PE today. Mom was really mad. I haven't been doing very good in school lately.*

> *MAY 22: Today I got two Unsatisfactories, one in science and English. I didn't show them to Mom (too scared).*

> *MAY 23: About the two Unsatisfactories I got yesterday—I forged Mom's name.*

In the accelerated classes, I was no longer with people I had known since kindergarten. I was shy and uncomfortable. I was angry with my parents when they spoke about my high-achieving cousin, Cathy. It seemed that they wanted me to be just like her.

> *JUNE 3: Sometimes I feel that nobody knows that I'm alive. I feel so alone.*

I wanted a boyfriend. I wanted to be in "the in crowd."

Occasionally, a limit was set at home. If I didn't come home from school when I was supposed to, I might be grounded. My phone calls were limited to two minutes. I was thirteen when I wrote that I might run away from home. When I was very young, I pretended to run away by hiding in the garage. I could hear my parents calling for me, and it felt good to know that they cared enough to want to find me, but I was also afraid of their anger for scaring them. Mom hit me when they found me.

During the summer of 1967, Dad had to go to a convention in

Chicago, so we drove to Illinois for a three-week trip that included visiting Mom's family. Aunt Phyllis and my cousins came, too. It is a trip we wouldn't have attempted while Mikey was at home. I have sweet recollections of tasting pecan pralines at a roadside shack, visiting cowboy-themed souvenir stores in Albuquerque, New Mexico. My cousins and I had never seen fireflies before, and we caught them in a jar then let them go. We kids slept on the screened porch of one of Mom's relatives. It was pitch black outside. We couldn't see anything but knew that the cornfields extended forever. The only light came through the kitchen door, and I could see my parents sitting around the table talking, laughing, and playing cards with friends and relatives. They seemed relaxed and happy here. It is a scene deeply imprinted in my memory, and I sometimes call upon it now on nights when I am unable to sleep.

I believe my parents pulled together for the trip, just as they had for many years since Mikey's birth. But, retrospectively, I realize our nuclear family was dissolving.

pierced

One day we parked the station wagon at the curb right in front of Mikey's unit. Normally we parked in a lot a short distance away, but the staff knew we were coming, and it would only take a minute to check Mikey out for a weekend at home. I waited in the car while Mom and Dad went inside to get her, then we settled in for the drive home. I sat up in the front with Dad, and Mom was in the back seat with Mikey.

We had not driven far, were still on the hospital grounds, when Mom said, "Slow down Jim, I think something's wrong." Dad pulled over to the side of the road, "What is it?"

"I don't know. Look at Mikey."

Dad and I both turned to look at the back seat and saw that Mikey was sitting on her haunches, her butt a few inches above the seat. She was shifting a bit from side to side. Mom touched her shoulder. "Sit down, Mikey." Mikey sat, following directions, but only for a second then raised her butt again. Her face, sounds, and body posture told us that she was apprehensive.

Dad drove to an area off the road where there was some privacy so Mom could examine Mikey. Mikey had had abscesses on her butt that were surely painful to sit on, but we had never seen her act quite like this.

Mikey was eager to cooperate when Mom helped her turn over to lie, fully extended, over Mom's lap. I switched the overhead light on and reached over the seat to help Mom pull Mikey's pants down. She held perfectly still while Mom looked at her buttocks. There were reddened areas over bony prominences, and healing abscesses on her hips, but nothing to explain her discomfort. Then Mom pulled her buttocks apart to look at her rectum. There, protruding through her perineum, the taut skin between her rectum and vagina, was a metal prong about a half-inch long. It appeared to be the sharp end of a bobby pin. The other prong was not visible. The only explanation was that someone had inserted the 2-inch bobby pin, curved end first, into her rectum. Instead of coming out, one of the prongs had completely pierced through her skin. "Son of a bitch," Mom said, her face tight and voice constrained. I sensed her quiet rage.

Dad leaned over and looked closer. I thought I heard a muffled sob. "Jesus Christ," he said. I was still.

There was no way to remove the pin safely without risking further injury. What I saw that day is imbedded in my memory and sometimes comes unbidden to torture me. We drove immediately to the infirmary. It was later suggested to us that Mikey had inserted the bobby pin herself. That was the usual response to Mikey's injuries. Never accept responsibility: the Camarillo code.

After nearly two years, my parents were finally able to get Mikey transferred out of the adolescent unit and away from her torturers. Regulations were bent in order to place her on a unit with adults. There would be many other units in the years to come.

Today, when the unwelcome images visit me, I see the other girls taking Mikey to a private place on the unit, someplace where the staff wasn't likely to interrupt. I see Mikey cooperating—holding still as she was told, turning over as instructed, and being a good girl. Only to be violated, then unable to tell anyone that she was hurt. Or maybe she had scratched or bitten someone and suffered the consequences of their retaliation. The hairpin was not necessarily the most painful or frightening thing to happen to Mikey. The burns may have hurt more. Did they hold the lit cigarette to her skin to see her flinch, to hear her cry out? I remember how she relaxed onto my mother's lap, feeling safe and trusting that Mom would make it better, but Mom could not keep her safe.

The hairpin put an end to any childhood innocence I may have been hanging on to. It showed me new depths of cruelty, the capacity people have for hurting each other.

perfect storm

One warm spring afternoon when I was in the eighth grade, I was sitting at a picnic table with Anne in the deserted courtyard of our junior high school. We were discussing how to spend the rest of our day.

Three boys walked our way slowly, still half a football field away. As they neared, we could see that they were a bit older than us. Each had dark hair, and wore jeans and a t-shirt. I didn't recognize them. They sauntered toward us while we continued our conversation. When they approached our table, we all introduced ourselves. They were all holding bottles of Coca-Cola. One stood a bit ahead of the others. "What are you girls doing today?" he asked.

"Not much," I responded. "How about you?"

"Not much. Just hanging around."

We chatted a little more. The two other boys were quiet, nodding and smiling when their leader spoke.

"What grade are you in?"

"Eighth," Anne replied.

The two background boys turned as though they were going to move on, but the first boy asked, "Hey, do you want to take a red?"

"What?" Anne asked.

He pulled a small foil packet from his front pocket. "These," he said as he unwrapped enough of the foil to expose four red capsules. "Reds."

"I don't know," I said. I had heard of reds. Sleeping pills. I knew some of my friends had tried them, and I was curious.

"They make you feel good. Relaxed."

The two boys who still hadn't said much each took one, swallowing them with soda. The keeper of the pills held one out to me. Anne and I exchanged looks: "Should we?"

There were no clanging bells or blinking red lights warning me that I was standing at an intersection. No hint that turning right would take me to Mr. Hardin's English class to diagram sentences and to first chair of the cello section in the school orchestra. There was no sign indicating that a left turn would take me down a winding, pot-holed road, although an often exciting one.

I turned left and took the capsule. It was a simple choice, like picking out my blouse that morning.

My memory of the events that followed is fragmented. I was in the backseat of a car. The boys must have offered to drive me home, a little over a mile. Anne probably walked the few blocks to her house. Did she take a pill, too? One boy was driving, and I sat in the backseat between the other two. The boy on my right was touching me lightly on my face, neck, and breasts. When I pushed his hand away, he withdrew it.

"Come on," he crooned as he reached toward me again. Everything was blurry and seemed to move in slow motion. I felt the other boy reach around my waist. I think I was too drugged to be afraid—but I knew I did not want them to touch me.

The next thing I remember was finding myself alone, in a hedge, with my feet sticking out onto the sidewalk. I didn't know how long I had been there. There was still a little light in the sky. The boys must have dumped me out of the car. I wasn't quite easy enough, not quite loaded enough. It took me a moment to get my bearings. I was just outside the campus. I knew a bus stop was only a half-block away. My clothing was intact, though I don't think I gave it a thought. I struggled to my feet, staggered to the bus stop, and held onto a pole to keep myself standing. The Number 8 ran close to my house, so I'd only have another half-block to negotiate after I exited the bus.

The house was dark when I entered. No one was home. After getting a quart bottle of OJ from the kitchen, I staggered a short distance to the nearest bed where I passed out.

The sun was up when I opened my eyes to see my parents staring down at me, looking very stern. Mom said, "We tried to wake you up." They had been unable to rouse me. I had spilled a trail of orange juice from the kitchen to the bed, compounding their confusion about what had happened to me. I doubt if drugs crossed their minds. Drugs were only beginning to emerge as part of the American subculture. I didn't smell like alcohol.

I mumbled something about being "really tired." I must have still had the benefit of their doubt when it came to risky or unexplained behaviors. If I had managed to stumble to my bed instead of my mother's, I would have avoided the confrontation entirely.

I began to spend Friday and Saturday nights at the Ice Palace, a skating rink, with my friends, including Anne. The first time I went, I was with Lydia. She was my age, with long brown hair. She lined her large brown eyes with a black Maybelline pencil. Her mom worked nights, so Lydia was free to do as she pleased.

A breeze of cold, dry air hit us when we entered the building. Everyone wore sweaters. Twinkling lights danced on the enormous white oval of ice, reflecting the large twirling mirror balls above it. Music played and couples, kids, and singles skated around the rink's perimeter, like roller derby but nice and slow. Some more experienced skaters did spins and fancier moves in the center. I sat on a bench to put on my rental skates, wobbled for a few feet on the rubber flooring, and held onto a rail to watch the skaters. They were having fun, but skating didn't look fun to me. I felt like I didn't belong. These people were straight, average, normal, nerdy, mainstream. I said "Let's go" to Lydia, who was standing at my side.

"Okay."

That was the last time we went inside. The real action for my friends and me was in the parking lot. Every weekend, we met up after dark, lit cigarettes, and planned our evening. Sometimes we stayed in the lot, sometimes we ventured out. There were usually five or six of us.

An older guy, Otis, was often around. He was about twenty-five, tall, dark-skinned, and slender. He had beautiful hands with long fingers and oval-shaped fingernails. He always wore dark clothes.

Otis wasn't part of our group, but we saw him every weekend and sometimes bought joints from him.

One night, four of us asked him to buy us some Old English 800 malt liquor at the store around the corner. When Otis returned to the parking lot with a brown paper bag, we gave him two cans for his trouble, leaving us one each.

I had tasted beer before and hated it. I much preferred the sips of bourbon and 7-Up that my cousins and I used to filch from our parents' drinks during a poker game when we were seven or eight. "You'll get higher if you chug-a-lug it down as fast as you can," one of the guys assured me, "and you'll hardly notice the taste." That sounded good to me.

There must have been a reason we didn't just drink the liquor right there in the parking lot. Instead we walked a half block to the Greyhound bus station. It's easy to go unnoticed in a Greyhound bus station—a plus for fourteen-year-old kids who plan to get drunk. There are usually plenty of people milling around and the ticket sellers are busy.

We went into the public bathroom and when Lydia and I were each locked in our stall, she called, "Ready?"

"Ready," I said.

We popped our cans and guzzled. I only noticed the taste for a second. About a fourth of the way through the can I wasn't sure if I could keep going without puking, but I was dedicated to getting as high as I could, so I pushed the thought from my mind and finished the can. Then I sat silently on the toilet and felt the warmth envelop my body. Something relaxed inside me. I liked it. I liked it a lot.

"Are you okay?" I heard from Lydia in the next stall.

"Yeah."

"We should go."

"Okay, let's go."

Even at a Greyhound bus station, there was some risk of drawing attention to ourselves. If adults came into the bathroom, they might notice the smell of alcohol or be able to tell that we were high. We wanted to get back to the street and on with our night.

We met up with the guys. "Well?" one of them asked me.

"It's great!" I replied.

We walked to the Santa Monica Pier a few blocks away. As long as we were back at the Ice Palace by 10:00 P.M., to be picked up by my dad, we could do whatever we wanted. The pier was bustling on Friday and Saturday nights, especially during the summer. We blended in with the couples on dates and the families with children. We played games in the arcade and accumulated tickets that we could use to purchase trinkets. We took pictures in the photo booths and ambled down the wooden planks to look out over the railing at the waves crashing on the shore.

Then we walked back to Ice Palace and waited on the benches in front so it would look like we had been skating. People were coming out to go home when my dad pulled up in our station wagon.

It didn't take long to learn that vodka gave me the same results as beer but faster. In a short time, I was drinking a half-pint an evening and was still able to appear sober. "Maintaining," keeping an aura of sobriety when intoxicated, was considered cool, and being cool was important to me. Lydia was my main drinking buddy for a few months until she got a boyfriend.

Mom continued to go out every night except when Mikey

came home. In the evenings, Dad spent his time in front of the television until I went to bed. Then he left to go to the Joker, a nearby bar, coming home around 2:00 A.M. He got irritated more easily. There was an unspoken rule not to upset him.

I don't think my parents noticed the changes occurring in my life.

Some kids carried heavy book bags, raised their hand in class, and ran for office. They were the ones whose parents had plans for them: college, maybe the family business, or marriage and family. They were the ones whose families had dinner together each night. Their lives looked calm and ordered. I could have fit into their world. But I was attracted to those who crossed the line of risk and non-conformity. I bonded with kids who lacked structure, whose parents were naïve, working, or indifferent. Many of my friends had single parents who left them unsupervised after school or at night. We didn't have plans for the future.

Left to our own devices, we experimented. We were bold. Instead of making calculated decisions aimed at achieving goals, we made uninformed choices, like tossing a coin. My parents and I hadn't discussed goals, like college, although the accelerated classes I had been enrolled in were college preparatory. No one was paying close attention to us, so there were few consequences.

I straddled a line. On one side, I was the good girl I had always been, completing catechism classes and helping with Mikey when she was at home. But when Mikey wasn't at home, I felt invisible. It seems like it should have been the reverse, but our family functioned best, and I felt I belonged, when we were responding to a crisis.

On the other side of the invisible line, I discovered the allure of being just a little bit bad and getting away with it. I didn't feel pressure to fit in with mainstream kids. It was more important to me to be cool than to be popular. I embraced the familiarity of being an outsider and the acceptance of my chosen peers. With drugs and alcohol I felt in control. I could be up, down, or numb. I had found an antidote to the bleak reality of Camarillo.

As time passed, college preparatory classes and the school orchestra held less sway for me. I became adept at forging both parents' signatures. It would have been easy to blame Mikey for all my behaviors. But that would have been a lie. It didn't stop me from sometimes using her to elicit sympathy from my teachers in order to lessen the consequences of one infraction or another.

I was in the middle of a perfect storm. Upheaval in the world around me coincided with upheaval in my life. In 1968, when I was fourteen years old, Bobby Kennedy and Martin Luther King were assassinated. The civil rights movement was gaining momentum, the Vietnam War raged on, and anti-war activism was spreading. Around the country, a counterculture was evolving that advocated non-violence and love. Young people were claiming their freedom from the status quo. Men grew their hair long. Women stopped wearing bras. Drugs, music, and relaxed sexual mores were all part of the cultural transformation. People living in the traditional world viewed these changes as an affront to their sensibilities. As a young girl without direction, it was easy to be influenced by the turmoil of the times. I was too young to be driving the bus of change, but I was an enthusiastic passenger.

david

My mother, father, and I were each scarred by the tragedy of Mikey and tormented by her circumstances at Camarillo. I don't begrudge my parents the escapes they found. We each paid a price for the choices we made in order to cope.

To be fair, my parents were not completely absent. Mom was often home in the afternoons when I got back from school. Dad tried to help me with my algebra, although he became irritable when I didn't get it. But we were seldom all together, except when Mikey came home or when we visited her at Camarillo. She was the axis around which our family turned, and in her absence all the wheels of what, for our family, was a normal life stopped.

My parents were naïve about the changing times and my opportunities for misadventure. They were accustomed to not worrying about me. And my adventures weren't too alarming in the beginning.

As my grades dropped, my parents received letters from school that I was unable to intercept. They learned about my truancy and lack of motivation. I bristled at the too-late attempts at oversight. As a child, I had been comfortable in the background. Now an adolescent, I was drawing attention to myself for all the wrong reasons, and I wanted my invisibility back. I didn't want to give up my freedom to choose whether I would go to class, who I spent time with, or what I did.

I was fourteen the first time I ran away from home. I thought of it as just not coming home rather than running away. It was Sunday, and as I was leaving the house to go to the beach with Anne, Dad told me to be home by 4:00 P.M. and that I couldn't go out that night. That day, Anne and I met two boys, runaways who were fifteen. They had come all the way from Chicago. We spent the day walking on the boardwalk and sitting on the sand, talking. When 6:00 P.M. rolled around, and I didn't want to face the ire of my father for being late, I decided not to go home at all.

"Tell my parents I am okay but you're not sure where I'm staying," I told Anne. "Tell them I will be home tomorrow." I didn't want her to be harassed for information.

"But you know they'll think I know where you are. They won't believe me."

"Just tell them."

"Okay."

As the sun went down and the air grew cold, I held John's hand, and we walked to the hotel where he and his friend were staying. The hotel was right on the boardwalk. Locals called it the Roach Hotel. It was an old building that had been painted blue at one time, but the paint was faded to almost white. The curtains in the windows hung sloppily. Inside, the halls were dark and the carpet threadbare. The rooms were grungy, each with one double bed and a tall dresser. Four boys were staying in the room. Only the two runaways from Chicago had known each other a week earlier. All were new to California. They were nice enough, friendly but not intrusive.

John had longish sandy hair and soft brown eyes. He was gentle, and I felt safe with him. We slept on the hard floor, sharing a pillow and thin blanket. We cuddled and kissed a little until we fell asleep. In the morning, we walked outside to a perfect day. The air was cool. The ocean mirrored the deep blue sky and sparkled under the bright sun. It was early. The lifeguard stations were unmanned and the beach was empty, with the exception of some noisy seagulls.

John didn't talk much about his home life. I don't know why he ran away. A lot of runaways came to Los Angeles, many finding their way to Venice and the Sunset Strip. I complained some about my parents. "I don't know why they are so strict. They don't know anything about me. They aren't around much anyway." We didn't talk about our plans for the future but sat quietly listening to the waves, then walking along the boardwalk and pier. I always knew that I would go home, but I had a feeling that John wouldn't. I slept on the hard floor with him for two more nights, our affection never progressing beyond kissing and cuddling.

Our time together was carefree. But I didn't have any money, and the boys didn't have enough to take care of me, too. I tired of living in the same clothes, a sandy bathing suit covered by jeans and a top. Before I went home, I told John that I would try to come back to see him. We hugged for a long time before I began my walk, only four blocks, to the Santa Monica Police Department.

I'm not sure why I took myself to the police department instead of just going home. I must have thought my parents had reported my disappearance, although they hadn't. Maybe I hoped that they would have wanted help to find me. A stern officer gave me a lecture and then I waited in a glass holding room for a couple of hours. When my parents arrived, they seemed more annoyed than worried. The car was quiet when we drove home, and they never asked where I had been.

I never saw John again. By the time I was able to return to the hotel to see him, all the boys were gone.

On the following Saturday, Mom informed me that I was going to accompany her that evening. She didn't tell me where we were going, but she wanted me to look nice, so I wore a knee-length, multicolored dress with long sleeves.

As we drove to Inglewood, about twenty minutes away,

she explained we were meeting a friend of hers. His name was David. We climbed a white stone staircase in a modest apartment building, and I stood a step behind her on the threshold as she rang the doorbell. The man who answered the door was not tall or short, maybe 5'9". Not fat or thin. He wore a plain white, long-sleeved shirt and dark trousers. His most remarkable feature was his thick, almost-black hair that he wore combed back. His hooded eyes were dark and his skin light olive. He looked a little like Humphrey Bogart.

"This must be Terry," he smiled, holding the door open. Then he looked up at Mom.

"Hello Marcile," he continued to smile.

"Terry, this is David," Mom said.

I said hello, wondering how he fit into Mom's life.

"Well, come on in, you guys," he opened the door wide.

I walked a little way into the apartment, not knowing what would come next.

"Sit down, sit down. Can I get you something to drink?" he asked. "I have some soda in the fridge."

"No. Thank you," I said, my eyes downcast. I sat on the dark green vinyl couch that faced a television on the opposite side of the room. A *TV Guide* and an ashtray were on the coffee table in front of me. Mom walked up to David and kissed him, a peck on the lips.

"Well, I'm going to put the kettle on for tea. Are you sure you don't want anything, Terry?" David asked.

"No, I'm okay. Thank you."

Wow. Wow. I didn't know that Mom had a boyfriend.

I never had a clue. Well, I suppose it was unlikely that she was playing poker every night until five in the morning, but I had never considered that she wasn't. It explained why she didn't always answer when I paged her at the card club to say goodnight. She must have been spending the night here with him, sleeping in his bed.

I wondered if my dad knew. I assumed that this was a

secret, and I was uncomfortable to be party to keeping it from him. A couple of years later, I learned that he had known. Maybe it explained why he paced the kitchen when he came home from the bar at 2 am, when the house was dead quiet. He didn't know I was watching when he stood at the sink, the window black with night, looking out at nothing for a long time. I was a little bit afraid of him at those times.

So began my forced participation in what I thought was a secret part of Mom's life. I kept her non-secret, never saying anything at home about David.

We watched TV for a couple of hours that first night, Mom sitting close to David while I sat quietly at the other end of the couch. Later, we went in David's blue Pontiac to his and Mom's favorite Mexican restaurant and had combination plates. I didn't say much. If David asked me a question, I answered it politely. I was shy unless I was with my friends.

It was still early in the evening when Mom and I returned home. Everyone acted as though nothing had changed, like it was just like any other day.

One night, Mom took me to the card club. The first thing I noticed upon entering was the sound of poker chips click-clicking as players made bets, fiddled with their stacks, or pulled their winning pot from the center of the table. About fifty poker tables were crowded into a large, smoky, brightly lit area that was two steps down from where we stood. Comfortable bucket chairs were placed behind the rail that divided the two sections of the room. It was darker here. Some players were lined up at cashiers' windows along the wall to cash in or buy chips. Mom asked a floor man to put her initials up on a chalkboard under 5 & 10 lowball. There were three or four people above her on the list.

Mom and David met here when he was a professional card player—a prop. Props are paid a stipend by the house to play in games that are shorthanded. Filling empty seats with props allowed the house to keep a table going when there weren't enough players. I learned that most of the players were regulars. Some had names like Dirty Shirt Johnny.

Each player paid an hourly collection to the Chip Girls that circulated through the card room. Mom had encouraged David to get a regular job, and when I met him, he was the manager of a Gallenkamps shoe store.

When the floor man called Mom's initials, she navigated her way through the maze of tables to her chair. Chip Girls brought drinks (no alcohol) and food to players. Not surprisingly, Mom soon had a cup of tea on a little table pulled close to her chair.

I continued to spend time with Mom and Dave, mostly when Dad was out of town. It was her way of babysitting me. Usually we watched TV at his apartment and ate out. Dave didn't play cards much now that he wasn't playing professionally, now that he had a regular job, but Mom still played. When she and I went to the card club, I sat in the outer circle and watched for a few hours. I enjoyed being on the periphery of this little subculture, outside the mainstream, with its whisper of affiliation with organized crime.

My relationship with Dad was tainted by my betrayal. I felt a gap between us because I kept Mom's secret and spent time with her and her boyfriend. Dad's naiveté about my lifestyle away from home marginalized him further. I still went to the Ice Palace, on the pretext of ice-skating, whenever I had the opportunity.

I knew Mom had met David at the card club, but I didn't consider how long she had been seeing him. Decades later, he told me that she "was really broken up when Mikey was committed. She cried and cried." I realized then that she had been seeing him while Mikey was still at home. Leaving Mikey, Dad, and me alone each night to play cards had never seemed like a betrayal. But leaving us to see David was different. My heart ached when I learned that she shared her grief and tears with him instead of with us.

mikey's bliss

It was hard to know if the pleasures of Mikey's visits at home outweighed the anguish of returning her to Camarillo. At home, she took long baths. She sat in her chair in the dining room, turning the handle on the jack-in-the-box so it played "Pop Goes the Weasel," and giggling when the lid flew open and the clown popped out. One of us stopped to push the little clown back down into the box so she could do it again and again. But there were still incidents of biting and head banging. Sometimes the entire stay was marred by violence.

She may have understood words in our conversations about returning to Camarillo because she seemed to know when the visit was coming to an end and began to make unhappy sounds. So we were careful about what we said. After we had arrived back at the adult unit, she clung and cried when we transferred her to staff. I can't help but visualize the times she reached her arms through the bars of the unit door when we were leaving, as though begging, "Don't leave me. Don't leave me." Sometimes the attendants treated her roughly, and we knew that her agitation would have consequences—a shove into a chair, harsh words, and a shot. Doctors rotated through the units, sometimes staying only a few months. Each new doctor put her on one of the major tranquilizers, one of the "-zine" drugs. Each time, she got worse until they finally stopped it. Then the next doctor would start the whole routine again.

To avoid such painful returns, we began to spend our visits on the hospital grounds. We were careful not to use the word "home," but if we slipped, Mikey lit up, anticipating the pleasures of being back in the house. We were robbing her of the only happiness she knew in order to protect her from institutional brutality. It was an imperfect solution.

The first time we took Mikey to the hospital's canteen, I waited in the car while Mom and Dad went to get her. Then Dad drove about a half mile to the huge administration building. It was the weekend, so the building was empty. Our steps echoed in the lobby. I carried a grocery bag full of food. Mom and Dad each held one of Mikey's hands as we went down the old elevator to the basement. The large, poorly lit room was painted dark tan and was empty when we arrived. There were round, white plastic tables with attached stools bolted to the floor. Three vending machines stood on one side of the room.

Mom led Mikey to a seat, and she began to rock quietly. I set the bag of food and utensils on an adjacent table. Sounds alerted Mikey to exactly what was happening and a smile spread across her face as she heard the rustling of paper. She reached her hand out. "Wait a minute, Mikey," Mom said, letting her know that food was coming soon. Mikey lowered her hand and waited. I opened cans and containers of food that we had prepared at home and began to place items on the plate: luncheon meat and wax beans. When Mikey heard the click of the plate being set down in front of her, she felt for the food and daintily picked up a piece of ham. One of the vending machines dispensed hot beverages: chicken broth, coffee, hot chocolate, or tea. I brought two cups of sweetened tea back to the table, one for Mom and one for Mikey, but they were too hot, and I put them aside for a while. As Mikey ate, I added strawberries and cantaloupe to her plate.

Another vending machine had little cups of vanilla ice cream, and Dad sat next to Mikey and fed some to her using a spoon we'd brought with us.

I kept everything organized and packed things back in the sack as the visit went on. That way we'd be ready to go quickly if Mikey's behavior deteriorated. We were lucky and had the room to ourselves for the entire visit.

After lunch, Mom and I took Mikey to the ladies room and inspected her for bruises and bites. The scars from cigarette burns were still visible, but there hadn't been new burns since she was transferred out of the adolescent unit.

It was a warm day, and we went for a little walk and sat on the grass. Mikey held the transistor radio that we'd brought next to her ear and smiled as she listened to the music and moved the dial.

She lay down, with her head in Mom's lap, and held still while Mom picked her blackheads and stroked her hair.

She wasn't as agitated when we returned her to her unit at the end of the visit as she had often been after a visit home.

peter and jim

I've told my close friends, "If I develop dementia when I get old, and I seem confused, ask me what year it is. If I say it is the summer of 1969, DO NOT try to re-orient me. DO NOT ask me if I know my name or who the president is. DO NOT attempt to bring me back to the present by saying, 'No, no, this is 2040 and you're in The Star Bright Nursing Home. I'm your friend Bev—don't you remember me?' Just crank up the volume on a Jimi Hendrix song and let me be." They chuckle, but I'm serious. Although 1967 was the official Summer of Love, mine was 1969, when I was fifteen, between junior high and high school.

Anne and I often arrived at Tree Park in Venice before noon. It was narrow, about a block long, and tucked away on a quiet residential street. The grass was thick and dark green. A couple of old trees with expansive canopies provided shade, and there were two or three picnic tables. Summer days were most often lovely, not too hot, and not too cool, with a subtle breeze that traveled from the ocean ten blocks to the west. Some days we arrived early, when the park was empty, but soon the twins would join us. Darryl and Dale were my age and identical: cute, blond, freckled. Those who knew them well could tell them apart. I think Dale had a gentle crush on me. We would stretch out on the ground on our backs, looking up through green leaves at the blue sky, our fingers barely touching. We occasionally spoke about the beauty of the sky or a walk to the beach, but mostly we were quiet. Gene might have been the next to arrive. He was Mexican-American, with thick curly hair, a laid-back manner, and a smile that always said, "I'm happy to see you." With an entire day ahead of us, we were in no hurry to make plans, content just to sit and talk. Peter and Tony often joined us. They were from England and a grade ahead of Anne and me. Tony had blond hair and big brown eyes while Peter was lanky with long brown hair. Their accents made them even more appealing. There were about fifteen regulars in the group of people frequenting the park.

As noon rolled around, we usually walked to the house next door where a pair of brothers lived. Anne had a crush on Frank and I had one on Anthony. They were older, twenty and eighteen. Every summer, their mother went to Italy, the old country, to visit family, leaving the house to them.

The dim living room was filled with heavy antique furniture. There was that not-unpleasant musty odor often found in old homes with aging rugs, curtains, and upholstery. *The Godfather* had not yet been made; the people in the old sepia photographs that hung on the dining room walls looked like the citizens of Corleone.

The house was the perfect place to gather, listen to music, and be with friends. There was usually a joint being passed around, but I didn't care for marijuana. I loved the cool nickname, "Irish," I had been given by one of the boys.

There was always music in the house and often a dozen or more people gathered. Several in the group were musicians and they played soft rock or blues on their guitars. The Moody Blues were often on the stereo.

"Lovely to see you."

When it was too beautiful a day to stay inside, we returned to the park.

I felt light, happy, and free. I felt like I belonged.

I knew my freedom was transient. I would have to return to school, but for almost three months I relished my independence and wished it could last forever.

Drugs and alcohol were part of the lifestyle I had chosen in junior high school, and I continued to drink and use uppers and downers. If Anne and I wanted to enjoy a buzz, we needed to start early. Although the summer days were long, it would take several hours until we were straight enough to go home. Darryl might pass around some Seconol capsules—reds. Too much and I had to struggle to stay awake, but in the right amount they made me feel calm, at peace, and without worry.

One day, I sat alone in a tiny garage that had egg cartons tacked to the walls and foam rubber stuffed in the gaps of the doors. I sat on a shabby worn sofa, closed my eyes and listened to Led Zeppelin on the stereo. In the still darkness, immersed in the sound of Jimmy Page's electric guitar, I learned that music could take me to the same place that drugs took me. It transported my body and mind to another dimension.

Some nights, late, Anne snuck out in her father's brown-and-white Plymouth station wagon and picked me up. Her parents had divorced, and all four daughters lived with their father. She was a poor driver. We flew over dips, landing with a thud. She didn't stop completely at stop signs and braked only when on top of a red light. But we were never pulled over, and our parents never knew about our escapades. We went to Anthony and Frank's house to spend a couple of hours in the smoke-filled living room. There were more people at night. A few were usually in the kitchen, where it was quieter and more conducive to conversation. Most were scattered around the living room.

When Independence Day rolled around, Anne and I headed to the beach. There was a long-standing tradition of partying and fireworks at the local beaches. Parking lots overflowed early. Throngs of people of all ages crowded the boardwalk. Families sat in groups on the sand, and children ran about waving sparklers.

Once night fell, explosions of colored light reflected on the ocean from Santa Monica's extravagant fireworks display.

Anne and I arrived at the Number twenty-two lifeguard station at around noon and headed south toward Venice, where a love-in was scheduled. There was a palpable change when, walking on the boardwalk, we crossed an invisible line between Santa Monica and Venice. The aroma of sweet, earthy incense, patchouli oil, and pot wafted from the open doors of head shops where madras skirts and tie-dyed t-shirts were for sale. A phonograph in one of the shops was turned up loud, and Janis Joplin belted out "Take Another Piece of My Heart."

Venice Beach was to Southern California what Haight-Ashbury or Golden Gate Park was to San Francisco. People in faded, patched jeans, the girls braless and wearing halter tops, ambled barefoot along the boardwalk. The sun shone on their tanned bare shoulders. Everyone wore his or her hair long. I wore hip-hugger jeans, a light t-shirt over my orange bikini, and Indian leather sandals. People smiled warmly, nodded, and said hello. They seemed happy. I felt at home here.

Live bands were playing at the pavilion and, as we expected, Anne and I saw quite a few people that we knew. The day passed, leisurely and warm, in the company of friends.

The sun was almost below the horizon as Anne and I strolled along the boardwalk, past Hot Dog on a Stick, back toward the Santa Monica Pier. We were loaded on reds. Tony and Peter, our English friends from Tree Park, were with us. Shortly after dark had descended, Peter asked me, "Do you ball?"

"What?" It sounded like he said, "Do you baw?"

"Do you ball?"

I hesitated. *Did he say ball?* Meaning to have sex.

My momentary confusion and sedation delayed my response, and he grabbed my hand and gently pulled me away. We walked on the sand together, silently, closer and closer to the pier. Anne and Tony lagged behind.

Under the pier, a cool, damp, saline breeze brushed my face

and arms. I could hear the ocean gently lapping the shore fifty feet away. A twenty-foot wide path between wood pilings was used for access between the north side and south side beaches. The sand was wet and packed hard. We stepped off and walked among more pilings into a darker secluded area where the sand was drier.

We were alone; Anne and Tony had not followed us this far. After we sat down, Peter leaned in to kiss me. I felt relaxed, an end of a hot day at the beach underscored by the effects of the drugs, and a little excited, because I liked Peter.

He mumbled something, cooing. With one hand supporting my back and one floating over my breasts, he slowly lowered me so that I was lying down. Soon he was fumbling at my jeans as he continued to kiss me. I whispered, "I'm a virgin."

He reached his hand down my bikini bottom, and I felt his fingers inside me. The fireworks display had begun and I heard the loud booms. I felt a twinge of pain, not too bad. Through the haze of seconol I thought: *I just lost my virginity*. Peter sat up and looked into my eyes with a surprised expression on his face. I think he was taken aback by the knowledge that he was my first. Fireworks were blasting in rapid succession—KABOOM, POP, CRACKLE. The air smelled of cordite as I pulled my pants up, gritty with sand, and got ready to leave. We joined Tony and Anne, who were sitting on the beach a few yards away. The air was smoky as the fireworks display continued.

When we separated, Peter said, with a tone of urgency, "I have to see you again."

Back at my house, Anne and I were in the bathroom, she on the edge of the bathtub as I sat on the toilet to pee. I was surprised when I saw the blood on my bikini bottoms. She saw it, too. "Oh, I must have started my period," I said, although I knew immediately that the blood confirmed that I had lost my virginity. We had often spoken about being "devirginized," wondering how and when it would happen. I felt torn between wanting my experience to be privately my own and feeling a little guilty that she and I had not shared the planning of it.

When it came to boys, and later men, Anne and I didn't let relationships separate us. Whether fantasy or real, our romances were usually with men who were friends or somehow related. It began with our girlish crushes on Beatles George and Paul; then we moved on to sixth-graders David and Allen. If I continued to see Peter, Anne would have seen Tony. There were more couples like this as time passed.

My first time was not romantic—no sexy lingerie, expensive wine, candles, or soft music. But there were, literally, fireworks. Sometimes I've wished that it had been with someone who loved me, and whom I loved back. But I also relish the fact that it was off the beaten path and spontaneous. I was glad that I had finally gone all the way—gotten the milestone over with.

Later that summer, Anne and I were riding in a car with Jim and a friend of his. I didn't know Jim well at all; he was just an acquaintance from Tree Park. He was eighteen, about six feet tall, solidly built, with medium-brown hair and eyes and a swarthy complexion. I had never met his friend. I had taken at least two reds and maybe some alcohol, too. Jim parked the car and led us to an apartment. When he opened the door, I staggered into the living room. "This belongs to a friend of mine," Jim said. "He said we could use it."

Anne and the second fellow, a nondescript skinny guy with messy, long blond hair, crossed the room and sat on a couch. I was disoriented but mentally clear enough to want to know the time. I was a little worried about getting home when I was expected.

I wandered around looking for a clock, eventually finding one on a nightstand in the dark bedroom. My vision was blurry, so I walked further into the room.

I felt Jim standing right behind me, and then he was pressing his body against mine. His breath was hot as he bent down to nuzzle my neck. Taking hold of my shoulders, he turned me around to face him then lowered me onto the large bed. I didn't want to have sex or even to kiss him, but my drugged body was limp and compliant.

His body was heavy on mine as he kissed me and began to undress me. "No, I don't want to," I said. He mumbled something I couldn't decipher. There were a couple of inches between his chest and mine, so I was able to raise my hands to his shoulders to try to push him away. But I was too weak. I was wearing my favorite jeans. They had a drawstring waist, and Jim was having a hard time removing them. He tugged and tugged. I yelled then, "Stop! Stop!" Eventually, he tore the jeans, splitting the seams, and pulled them below my knees, all the while holding me down with his torso. He was silent as he unzipped his fly and pushed his hard penis against me. My muscles contracted automatically, trying to keep him out, but he forced himself into me. It hurt, and I cried out. There was no point in struggling anymore. I lay back, trying to relax my muscles to reduce the pain, and waited for it to be over. After a couple of minutes of thrusting, he was finished. I could feel the buttons of his shirt pressing into my chest.

In a moment, he got up, zipped his pants, and reached out to take my hand, helping me up from the bed. I stood and pulled up my pants, saying nothing. He said, "Let's go out to the living room and see how those guys are doing." He acted as if nothing unusual had happened, so I did, too. I just wanted to get out of there and go home. I followed him into the living room where Anne and the other fellow were sitting on the couch kissing. Jim continued to act nonchalantly as we left the apartment, then he dropped Anne and me off at my house.

"Why didn't you come to help me? Didn't you hear me yelling?" I asked Anne.

"I thought you were having fun." Her answer didn't make sense. How could "no" and "stop" sound like fun? I didn't pursue it. I didn't say anything more.

Later, when I was alone, I thought to myself, *What should I expect?* After all, I had walked into the bedroom, and I was loaded. *Did I lead him on?* He probably thought I wanted to have sex with him. Maybe he believed that "no" doesn't mean "no." *I shouldn't be surprised by what happened,* I told myself.

"Free love" was emerging as the norm in the late 1960s sub-culture that I wanted to belong to. In my mind, casual sex was just part of the lifestyle and I should get comfortable with it. *No big deal,* I thought.

I didn't expect intimacy or pleasure in my ensuing sexual encounters. I wanted to become good at sex but it was painful. I clenched my muscles involuntarily. My body hadn't been able to keep Jim out but it was determined to prevent further intrusions.

Years later, when I heard the term "date rape," I felt sad for the girl I had been back then. Jim had overpowered me and taken what he wanted, but I had accepted responsibility for it.

acid

The summer of '69 had more in store: Woodstock, the Manson murders, man's first walk on the moon, and I ran away from home again. There were no particular problems. My parents and I went our own way most of the time. But they seemed convinced that my new friends were a bad influence. I went to Venice, which was rougher than Santa Monica, to spend time with them rather than bringing them home. When my parents decided to curtail my freedom, telling me I couldn't go to the park, I rebelled. I put together a few changes of clothes and showed up at Anthony's house. He and Frank welcomed me, but I posed a dilemma for them. They were over eighteen and surely they could get in trouble for harboring a minor. I was immature and didn't consider that it might become an issue.

Everyone was excited about the moon walk. The television was broadcasting the news in the living room, but Anthony and I sat together on the kitchen steps that led to the backyard. It was a clear night and we were looking up at the moon. I thought about the millions of people around the world who might be looking up and watching at the same time.

The nightly news was usually filled with stories about the

war in Vietnam—guerilla warfare, body bags, the Tet offensive, My Lai, napalm, villages burned. The moon walk seemed to represent something unifying and uplifting in a world torn apart by the war between democracy and communism. Vietnam had not yet touched me personally. Most of my friends were too young to enlist or be drafted. I embraced the cultural changes—the music, drugs, peace, and love, but I was naïve about anti-war protests and politics in general.

I slept next to Anthony that night. He kissed me a little and we went to sleep.

On my second evening, there were fifteen or more people crowded into the living room and the adjoining dining room. Several blues musicians, black and older than the rest of us, were there, jamming with Anthony and some others. I was sitting on a sofa in a quiet part of the room, drinking wine from a large green jug, passing it to Dale next to me. Someone asked if I wanted some acid. Most of my Tree Park friends were experienced with LSD, but this would be my first time. With Dale's input, it was agreed that I would take half a tab.

Established next to Dale, drinking wine, I waited to feel the acid. I didn't know what to expect. "Sometimes it takes a while," Dale said after about twenty minutes. I drank some more wine and waited another half hour. Still nothing. "This is not working; I think I should take some more." I took another half.

Shortly after the second pill, I began to see pale, pastel, kaleidoscopic patterns on the wall next to the couch. The colors moved slowly. Then the wall seemed to breathe, bulging gently out from the center then returning to flat, in and out. "Wow," I said.

Dale asked, "Are you coming on?"

"Yeah." I watched the wall, mesmerized by the moving patterns of color. It was beautiful.

"Do you feel okay?" he asked.

"Yeah."

We sat quietly. The intensity of my hallucinations increased as the additional acid I had taken began to take effect. I looked

down at my hand resting on my leg and could see the blood flow-
ing through my veins.

I went into the bathroom and made the mistake of looking
in the mirror. I don't know how long I stared at a single pore that
grew larger, darker, and deeper before I finally retreated to the
bedroom where I hid under a blanket waiting for the trip to end.
Someone pulled the blanket back to ask if I was okay. His huge,
piggish head seemed to be inches from mine, and dark blood was
running through his veins. "Yes," I mumbled. Back under the
safety of the blanket, I waited it out, telling myself that it would
all go away when the acid wore off.

Everything was better the next day. The sun was shining
and Dale and I sat together on a couch on the front porch. The
quiet street was in front of us, and Tree Park was visible to our
left. The kaleidoscope of colors was gone, and only mild distor-
tions of movement remained. "Do you see trails?" Dale asked as
he waved his hand slowly in front of my face.

Just at that moment, I saw my parents driving slowly in
front of the house, looking for me. I jumped up, ran to the car,
and got in. It was important that no one get into trouble because
of me, so I went along willingly. Someone must have alerted my
parents to where I was staying.

I don't recall the legal process that landed me on probation.
My parents didn't take me to the police station, but they must
have sought help from the authorities to control me or to scare me
into complying. Within a month, I was mandated to check in for
monthly meetings with my probation officer, Mrs. Sheldon, who
sat at a cluttered metal desk in a large room filled with more cluttered desks. We exchanged few words. Once I told her I was doing
well, she seemed as eager as I was for our meetings to end. I was
also mandated to attend counseling. Mrs. Eberhardt, my social
worker, had an office in a small, homey brick building with a sign
in front: "Santa Monica Family Services." The inside was the
exact opposite of the sterile environment of the probation department. There were upholstered chairs instead of folding metal ones.

The light was candescent rather than fluorescent. It looked like it may have once been a home, later converted into offices. There were two or three small rooms used for individual meetings and a larger room for group meetings. I began with a sulking resentment at being expected to disclose my personal thoughts and feelings. I felt certain that it was a trick designed to report my activities to my mother or other authorities. Mrs. Eberhardt was middle-aged, a little plump. She had what I can only describe as a sparkle in her eye and seemed genuinely pleased to meet me. It didn't take me long to like her and eventually to begin to trust her. I could tell that she listened, really listened, to me. She waited until I finished talking and asked me questions without making me feel interrogated. I began to feel that she had my best interests at heart.

One session stands out above all others. I wasn't planning to say the things I did. I hadn't been waiting for the right time. We were having a seemingly benign conversation. She must have said something or asked me a question that elicited my response. "I feel like I'm supposed to make up for everything, for Mikey and their marriage, because I'm normal. I'm supposed to make it all worthwhile." I went on to tell her that my parents had never said this directly to me but that I thought it is what they had hoped for. It is why I was born. My words surprised me. I don't know if I had ever formulated these thoughts before, yet they came rushing out. As I spoke them, I knew that I believed them, too. I believed that I owed a debt for the good fortune of being normal. Not only had I failed to make things better, but I had also succeeded in making everything worse. I couldn't look Mrs. Eberhardt in the eye when I spoke but instead looked at a poster on the wall behind her desk. I felt guilty for telling her, felt as though I was betraying my parents.

She responded, "I think that if you feel this way, that there is truth in it." I sensed no judgment in her voice but calm confidence.

I must have been holding my breath, because it seemed to come out in a whoosh as I relaxed. I looked at her, flooded with relief. And surprise.

I began to sob then and told her that I felt it was too much to expect, unfair, an impossible task. I felt that I had let everyone down. Looking back, I can understand why the allure of freedom was so appealing to me. Had I been looking for an escape from the onus of their expectations—*let me be?* Or was I rebelling against them—*fuck you?* I know now that it wasn't that simple.

Mom saw Mrs. Eberhardt, too. Dad didn't go. Talking about feelings just wasn't something he was ever able to do. He became increasingly marginalized in the family. I think Mom's meetings with Mrs. Eberhardt, while sometimes about me, were often about her own unhappiness.

I was allowed to go to the park to see my friends sometimes. Maybe the agreed-upon approach was to allow me enough leeway so I wouldn't run away again. I suspect Mrs. Eberhardt had a role in it.

food

Mikey had been at Camarillo nearly four years. She was transferred to several different units. One didn't seem much different than another, and they all had a charge nurse who said, "She doesn't belong here." Who knew that better than we did? Mikey wasn't being helped; she and other patients were in danger there. No one seemed to have any idea how to care for someone who was so developmentally disabled, someone who couldn't communicate her needs and was blind. Mom and Dad tried, over and over, to make someone see that Mikey would do better in a quiet unit, if one existed. The vicious cycle of new doctors and medications continued. She always had bites. It was impossible to know the source of her bruises.

Mikey had always been slender, but she became noticeably thinner. I doubt anyone took the time to cut food up for her or tell her what was on her plate. She was expected to use utensils rather than touch her food and pick it up with her fingers. Soft-serve institutional food—oatmeal, mashed potatoes—would have been impossible for her to pick up even if she had been allowed. No one knew what she meant when she held out her hand.

We started bringing her home again, to feed her. She stuffed herself there, grabbing everything quickly off her plate, stuffing it into her mouth until her cheeks puffed out, then swallowing quickly. We filled her plate again. She seemed desperate to get as much as she could into her mouth before someone took it away.

She couldn't consume enough calories on a weekend to compensate for the lack at Camarillo, and her weight continued to drop, so we began to take groceries to her unit. We made it as easy for the staff as we could. Nothing needed to be heated or cut up. Canned cherries (we included a can opener), canned hominy, cardboard boxes of juice, peanut butter wafers, sliced luncheon meat. Nutrition would be nice, but calories were critical. We suggested that they put her in a quiet place and put some of the food on plastic plates that we provided.

Her weight continued to drop. It seemed that she had given up. I believe her world had become so unsafe, so horrible that she had become unable to function.

When her weight dropped to sixty pounds, her bones protruded sharply. Her back was red and bruised from rocking against her vertebrae. She was apathetic, weak, and couldn't walk steadily. Her cheeks were sunken, and her lips were parched from dehydration. Perhaps it would have been humane to let her die of starvation and dehydration. My parents brought her declining condition to the attention of the unit manager and the doctors many times. Finally, she was admitted to Camarillo's medical hospital, which was located on the grounds. I can't imagine why it took so long for her doctors to admit her. Did they just not see what was in front of them to see? What happens to patients with no one to stand up for them?

Mikey was discharged from the hospital after a week and returned to her unit. She had been given IV fluids to rehydrate her, but she was still weak and emaciated. She needed food. But she refused to eat. Her trust had been destroyed—and her will.

I was never required to accompany my parents on visits to see Mikey, but I usually went along. There was no tension between my parents and me on visits. If she had been doing well,

I would have gone less often. Her decline was critical, and I tried to help.

I tried to work my magic, as I had done when giving her medications at home. One day, we brought a lot of her favorite foods with us, found a quiet and shady picnic bench on the grounds and began to unpack the goodies. Mikey sat passively at the table. In the past, the sound of tearing cellophane alerted her that someone was opening a package that might contain a peanut butter wafer or some other treat. She would reach out tentatively or feel her plate if she heard something put on it. But this time she sat quietly—her hands down.

"Would you like some juice, Mikey?" I held a small carton of apple juice with a little straw in front of her. She seemed uninterested. "Here Mikey, take a sip." I touched the straw to her lips. She pursed them tightly, pulling her head back. I rolled up a piece of thinly sliced luncheon meat, hoping that the novel shape would entice her to try it. I told her what it was as I handed it to her. She took it and set it on the table. "Are you sure, Mikey? You like ham. Please try it."

She picked it up, brought it to her mouth, and set it down again. After trying cantaloupe unsuccessfully, we abandoned nourishment and went for empty calories—candy—anything to entice her to accept food. Nope. Not that day. We were helpless.

We were packing up, getting ready to return Mikey to her unit. She was stretched out in the backseat of the car. Not quite ready to give up, I handed her a roll of meat. "Please take this, Mikey." She took it from me, smelled it, tasted it—and she ate it! I think it had something to do with the familiarity and safety of the car. Or maybe she thought we were taking her home. I rolled up another slice, and she accepted that one too. It was a relief for all of us, but her future was uncertain.

Mom, Dad, and I talked on the way home. We wondered if she understood death, if she was committing suicide.

The staff on the unit seemed to begin to pay more attention. They allowed Mikey to sit quietly alone in the dining room after the others had finished their meals so she could eat the food that we brought for her, and let her use her fingers.

Doctors rotated in and out. They didn't seem to be around long enough to make much difference. I think the unit directors had the most control. I can imagine them saying to their supervisors, "Get that girl off my unit before something awful happens." Nearly starving to death might be what got Mikey transferred to a unit that was populated by older women who had been heavily medicated and institutionalized for decades. They were passive and moved with shuffling gaits. Lost in the fog of drugs or their personal psychosis, they were incommunicative and sat in chairs most of the time. Mikey was safer here, and we were relieved. She continued to bite herself and bang her head but perhaps a little less frequently. There were fewer noxious stimuli to agitate her, but there wasn't any positive stimulation either. She sat in her chair. Would this be her sentence for the rest of her life?

runaway

Meanwhile, back in the outside world, Mrs. Eberhardt had mediated a truce between my parents and me, and we were getting along well. I wasn't unhappy at home. Although I had a bedroom in the house, I had converted a small area in the garage into a space that felt more like my own. I surrounded my small sleeping area with hanging Indian bedspreads and filled an old cedar chest with clothes. Record albums and books were scattered here and there.

I had no inclination to run away again—that is, until Anne called me early in the morning of October 15, 1969. She shocked me when she said, "I'm running away. Do you want to come?"

This wasn't like her. She had been content living at her father's house. Our late night joyrides had gone undetected, and her behavior hadn't raised any red flags or drawn unwanted attention. Her dad worked hard, raising four daughters alone, and he seemed even-tempered.

"Why, what's wrong?" I asked her. She was furious with her father after a prolonged argument. My history of running emboldened her, and it was so easy for one of us to entice the other into an adventure.

"We could go up to San Francisco and find Hawaiian Paul (a friend from Tree Park) or stay at Noel's," Anne said.

Noel was our most hippie-like friend. Her mother was an artist and had moved, with her three daughters, to Carmel, the small coastal town in Northern California known as a haven for artists. Noel had invited us to stay, though we hadn't discussed the circumstances that visiting might entail.

"Are you sure about leaving?" I asked.

"Yes, are you coming with me or not?" She sounded firm in her resolve.

I thought that she just might go by herself, and I couldn't have that—she wouldn't be safe, I would worry about her, miss her, and miss out on the adventure. I couldn't resist.

"Okay. Let's go."

"Let's meet on the bus—in an hour," she said. With nothing better than a paper bag to carry my things, I began to collect essentials. In addition to the clothes I was wearing, I brought another pair of jeans, two or three tops, a warm coat (it was cold up north), and some socks and underwear. The cowboy boots I had on were the only shoes I needed. Eventually, we would need something better than brown paper bags for our belongings, so I stuffed a vintage bedspread into the sack that I could later sew into satchels. What to do for money? I went into the house and tiptoed into Mom's room. She was asleep. I opened the top drawer of her bureau and helped myself to a dozen silver dollars—souvenirs from trips to Vegas. Some were from the 1920s and 30s, but I didn't know they were valuable. I brought several albums that I thought I might be able to sell, Janis Joplin, Spirit, the Mammas and Papas, and Jimi Hendrix.

Then I took a minute to begin a letter I would send to my parents later. I called Dale, my Tree Park friend, to tell him that I would write soon and to ask him to mail the letter to my parents for me. I wanted it to be postmarked locally so they wouldn't know where I was. He confirmed that our friend Hawaiian Paul was still in San Francisco and that maybe we would be able to find him.

The house was still asleep when I slipped out the front door. Looking back, I see how cruel it was to leave without a note. At that time, I didn't ponder how my parents' worry for me, again, would compound the pain they already had to endure because of Mikey. I needed time to get far away before they began to look for me. They wouldn't realize that I had run away until late that night. First, I wouldn't come home from school, and then it would seem that I had stayed out late. When I didn't appear by morning, they would be afraid. I would be hundreds of miles away by then.

Anne was waiting at the bus stop as planned. As soon as she sat down next to me, we began to discuss what our next step would be. We wanted to arrive with a couple of hours of daylight remaining. We couldn't know how long it would take to get a ride once we stuck out our thumbs or how many rides we would need.

It was after 10:00 A.M. when we arrived at the spot on Pacific Coast Highway where we had chosen to begin our trip. With our paper bags on the ground at our feet, we stuck our thumbs out. I had long, brown, sun-streaked hair parted down the middle and wore bell-bottom jeans, cowboy boots, a handmade Madras top, and a thin leather choker with a single multicolored bead. Anne wore an identical top. She had curly blond hair and wore gold wire-framed glasses and an abalone choker. We hoped to attract a ride with someone like our Tree Park friends.

After we'd been standing in the hot sun for about an hour, a faded blue Volkswagen van pulled over onto the shoulder. A Volkswagen van was a good sign. We walked up to the passenger window. The driver was a slender guy, about twenty-five years old, with long blond hair. "Where are you going?" he asked us.

Anne responded, "Carmel."

"OK. I can take you all the way if you want."

"That's great!"

We picked up our bags of clothing and albums, climbed into the back seat, and pulled the sliding door closed.

It was an amicable trip. His name was Paul. He offered a

hit off his joint, but we refused. I still didn't like pot. He didn't say anything about two fifteen-year-old girls hitching to Carmel and San Francisco. It wasn't all that uncommon in 1969—at least not in our circle of friends. Anne and I talked about how we would get by in the long run. We would probably look for jobs taking care of someone's kids and cleaning house. We felt confident. We probably couldn't get regular jobs, considering our age and circumstances. Clearly, we were planning to stay away.

After several hours, Paul pulled off the road at the Big Sur Inn, a two-story cabin-like building, barely visible from the highway, tucked into the forest. The first thing I noticed when getting out of the van was the forest smell that washed over me, fresh green and pine. The air was cool and damp. Tall, crowded trees dripped water and obscured the sky. Untouched nature. Magnificent. Pine needles crunched under our feet as we walked to the inn. The smell of wood burning in a potbellied stove permeated the room.

A young woman was drying a plate with a towel and called out a friendly, "Hi Paul." She came over to hug him, and then called to her husband, "Paul's here!" Paul introduced us to Eileen and Tom. I got the impression that he traveled between San Francisco and Los Angeles frequently and this was one of his regular stops. While the three of them visited, Anne and I enjoyed hot coffee and apple pie. Tom and Eileen were warm and outgoing, asking about our plans and never commenting on our age. Everything—the room, smell, warmth, and people—blended into an unforgettable experience and a feeling of peace that I would look for again and again.

It was dusk when we arrived in Carmel. Paul left us across the street from the address we had for Noel. We thanked him for the ride and assured him that we would be all right.

"Okay," he smiled. He drove off to continue his trip north.

It was immediately apparent that our arrival at Noel's was problematic. "You can't stay here," she said. "I can't tell my Mom that you're here."

"But where are we going to stay?" I asked.

"I'm sorry. I have some friends that might be able to take you. They'll be coming up here later tonight."

We gathered the paper bags that we had concealed in nearby bushes, telling Noel that we would return in a couple of hours as she had instructed.

"Now where?" Anne said. It was dark, getting cold, and had begun to drizzle.

"I don't know, but we have to find a dry place." The drizzle was turning to rain; the albums would be ruined, and my paper bag was beginning to fall apart. We didn't know our way around, and we were afraid that we would stand out as runaways in the small town. After walking a short distance, we found a moderately sheltered spot under some bushes and trees. It was private, a few yards from the road near an empty field. If Noel's friends didn't work out, we would spend the night here.

We estimated that two hours had passed and ventured out of our shelter and back to Noel's house. An old dark-blue sedan was parked in front and Noel was talking with a couple of guys. She introduced us to Pete and Paul. Another Paul! They appeared to be about eighteen years old. "You can stay with them at Lise's cabin," she said. "At least for tonight."

"Sure, you can come with us," said Paul. "No problem." We stood under the porch light, and I could see that he was about eighteen, maybe a little bit older, slender, with wavy brown hair and deep brown eyes. Pete looked the same age and had straight blond hair.

The fog was rolling in. "We'd better get going before it gets worse," Pete said. The winding Pacific Coast Highway was treacherous in the fog. So we piled into the car, said "good-bye" to Noel, and set out for Big Sur.

We drove slowly due to the low visibility. Paul told us a little bit about Lise, the woman who was letting us stay at her cabin. She didn't know we were arriving with Pete and Paul, but they assured us that it would be fine. "She's kind of quiet," Paul said.

"Don't take it personally if she doesn't seem too friendly. It's just the way she is. She's a really good woman." Pete told us they had been staying with her for several months.

After about thirty minutes, we made a left turn onto a paved road called Palo Colorado. The pine trees were dense, forming a canopy above the road that even the fog couldn't penetrate. The only light came from our headlights. About a half-mile in, we arrived at Lise's cabin. "Come on in," Paul said. "Watch out for the banana slugs." There were a couple of four-inch-long, fat yellow slugs slithering along the wood porch rail. We followed Paul up a few steps onto the porch then entered a large room with a crackling fire burning in a stone fireplace. A beaten-up sofa faced it. A couple of equally beaten-up armchairs were placed haphazardly. Several wood chairs were pulled up to a square wood table in one corner. A pair of twin mattresses on the floor were pushed against opposite walls.

Lise was in her twenties and looked like Grace Slick, with dark curly hair and pale skin. It was Big Sur/San Francisco etiquette in those days to house runaways or other travelers as they passed through, and our friendship with Noel was our character reference. Lise stood with her arms crossed and a somber face. Pete and Paul had warned us she was aloof, but after a few minutes she began making tea and pointed out mattresses in the corner of the cabin where we could sleep.

It was wonderful to be in a warm, dry room and to put our belongings down. After about thirty minutes, there was a knock on the door. A slim man named Marco, with unkempt shoulder-length hair, matching beard and wire-framed glasses, had come over to ask who was going to Esalen. It must have been about 11:00 P.M. when we piled into the old blue sedan with Pete, Paul, and a neighbor. Lise stayed home. Marco drove another car and brought a few people from his house.

It took almost two hours to get to Esalen, about twenty miles south. I didn't ask about Esalen; I guessed I would find out soon enough. "They let locals use the baths at night," Pete told us. We parked and followed him down a narrow, serpentine path, lit only by the bright moon, and into a quiet, candle-lit, sulfur-smelling room that sat on cliffs overlooking the rugged Pacific shore. Everyone had taken or was taking off their clothes and stepping into large, hot, steaming mineral baths; several people occupied each stone bath. I had never been naked around a bunch of naked strangers, let alone in a tub with them, but as I slipped off my clothes, no one seemed interested in my nudity. People spoke softly if at all. There seemed to be a reverence for the privilege of being here and respect for the people who shared it. When I became too hot to stay in the water, I got out and stretched out on my stomach on a narrow table used for massage. The ocean-facing wall of the building was open and, as I listened to the waves below, a fine, cool ocean spray, or maybe it was fog, settled on my hot skin. The long day, hot water, and peaceful vibe all contributed to my feeling more relaxed than I ever had. I let go of all tension and worry. At that moment, everything was okay.

After a couple of hours, we dressed for the drive home. The fog was worse—there was no visibility at all. I knew it would be a dangerous ride back to the cabins. Fortunately, our drive was not on the ocean side of the highway, making it less likely that we would go off the road and over the cliffs. But if there were oncoming cars, they wouldn't be able to see us any better than we could see them. Hopefully, at 3:00 A.M., there wouldn't be anyone else on the road. Paul drove our car and took the lead, while Marco's car followed as close to our bumper as possible, using our red taillights as a guide. We inched along. Paul opened his door, looking down to see the line on the road while steering the car. On one of the turns, the back door swung open, and Anne tumbled out of the car onto the highway. The door hadn't been properly latched. She got up quickly. "I'm fine." She had an abrasion on her arm that was oozing a little blood but didn't seem to be seriously hurt. It was fortunate we had only been driving about five miles an hour.

Finally, we were back at Lise's. The sun would be up soon. Exhausted, I slept next to Paul on his narrow mattress.

coming home

I slept like a rock, waking late in the morning. The cabin was dim. The climate and dense foliage kept the canyon dark, cool, and damp. A fire burned in the fireplace, and Pete, Paul, and Lise were sitting around the table drinking coffee. Anne and I joined them, and began to discuss our next steps. We still planned to go to San Francisco but needed to get organized. Lise never said anything about how long we could stay or how we should contribute, but I got the feeling that she was a bit worried about having runaways staying with her.

The first order of business was grocery shopping. The proprietor of the local market agreed to give us two dollars for each silver dollar. Knowing that we had to conserve our funds, we decided that peanut butter and honey would provide us with the most nutritious bang for our buck and bought a large jar of each along with some crackers. Later, Lise bought my albums for two dollars each.

I spent the evening cutting up the bedspread I had brought and sewing sacks that Anne and I could use to carry our belongings. They were purple, the size of pillowcases and could be closed with a drawstring. That night, while we were sleeping, someone ate most of our peanut butter and honey while they tripped on acid. We didn't begrudge them; after all, food had been generously shared with us.

Anne moved to the cabin down the road and stayed with Marco. They looked like they belonged together—both slight, thin wavy hair the same length, wire-framed glasses, soft-spoken. There was a goat on Marco's property that provided milk for the few people who lived there. The goat looked a lot like Marco, or Marco looked a lot like the goat, which was apt: Marco was a Capricorn, the sign of the goat!

I spent time during the days sitting alone, looking out over the ocean. After running away from home three times, I knew that I would likely be sent to foster care if I returned, so it didn't seem like an option. Regardless of my improved relationship with my parents, I was in the legal system now, and there wasn't any wiggle room. I added to the letter that I had begun to my parents:

I know it's hard for you to forgive me for what I'm doing, but please try. I know too that this hurts you a lot, and the last thing I want to do is hurt you because I love you both very much. I haven't really done anything bad to run away for. I really am sorry about the past hassles we've had. I don't know what to say. I can't get my thoughts straightened out in my head, let alone put them down on paper. I'm going to miss you more than anything. For once I'm not doing something out of rebellion. Try to stay in good health and give Mikey a kiss for me. I promise I'll try to keep my head and do the right thing. I'll always love you. And try to believe that I'm not doing this to hurt you. Try, if you can, to have a little faith in me.

Love Forever, Terry.

P.S. Please take care of Princess. I'd hate to think that strangers were taking care of her. I don't want either of you to be unhappy.

Two days later, I added more:

Mom & Dad,

You don't know how much I miss you. I want to come home, but I'm afraid to. I'm a long way away from home. I can't believe myself, the first two times I ran away I didn't want to come home, but now it's all I think about. I'm fine. I've been good and haven't done any crazy things like I usually do. I'm not on any dope at all so don't worry about that. I know, more than ever before, how much I love you and need you. Anne is fine but not homesick like I am. Please don't worry about me. I'm really taking good care of myself. I hope you're taking good care of yourselves, because I'm worried about you.

Love, Terry

I mailed the letter to Dale, as agreed, so that he could re-mail it to my parents. I discovered it among my mother's things forty years later, postmarked a week later.

We had the name and address of a woman in San Francisco named Flo. She might know where our friend Paul from Tree Park was. Hitchhiking, it took us a few hours to get to her house at Stanyan and Waller in the Haight. We stood on Flo's porch with our purple bags at our feet and knocked on her door. It opened as far as the chain lock permitted, and a man said to us, "Nothing's happening" and began to close the door.

"Wait! We're looking for Hawaiian Paul. Is Flo here? Pete gave me this address," I said.

"Nothing's happening." The door closed.

We thought that maybe the people inside had been busted for drugs and didn't want anything to do with strangers. Or maybe they were high on meth and paranoid. In reality, the Manson murders, methamphetamine, and the violence at the music festival at Altamont marked the beginning of the demise of the hippie counterculture. Some escaped to communes to pursue their dreams of peaceful coexistence, but the sweet, hopeful innocence of the heyday of flower children was passing. I will be forever grateful that I experienced a little bit of it at a time when I was also hopeful and innocent. In spite of all the changes to come and the adulthood I grew into, my happiest memories are triggered on a warm day, in bare feet and faded jeans, when I smell a whiff of patchouli or hear a Janis Joplin refrain.

The vibe on the street in Haight Ashbury was not friendly. There were no hippies. We saw pick-up trucks with men in the back who watched us as they passed by. The only reasonable thing to do was to hitch back to Big Sur. The trip was relatively uneventful, with the exception of waiting over an hour for a ride at a freeway onramp in Santa Cruz. It was dark when we arrived at the cabin.

San Francisco had been a bust, and we hadn't developed a plan B. We could stay with our newfound friends, at least for a while. We still had some money and did not have to pay for lodging. Paul and Pete had each asked me to be their old lady. Anne and Marco would stay together. I loved the splendor of Big Sur: spending days in the beauty, peace, and quiet of the shady canyon; finding gaps in the dense trees that revealed a circle of deep blue sky and allowed brilliant rays of sun to warm a porch or a backyard; Blind Faith playing on a stereo; a cozy cabin or Esalen at night.

Just as in the previous times I had run away, people treated me with kindness, generosity, and respect. But I wanted to go home. Anne wanted to stay but not without me, so the day after we returned from San Francisco we said our goodbyes. Anne and I stuck our thumbs out on southbound Highway One. We had spent five nights away. After about twenty minutes, we got a ride all the way home from another kind hippie in a blue Volkswagen van. The house was dark and empty when I arrived at about 11:00 P.M.

Running away again was a violation of my probation and I had to face the consequences.

In December, a petition was filed with the L.A. County
Superior Court saying:

"Said minor resides with her parents and is beyond the control of such persons in that on or about 10/15/69, minor ran away
from home and remained away until on or about 10/20/69, at
which time she returned home."

At a hearing on January 20, 1970, I was *"adjudged and
declared a ward of the court under Section 601 of the Juvenile Court
Law. Custody of minor is taken from the parents and guardians and
minor is committed to the care, custody and control of the Probation
Officer for suitable placement."*

I was permitted to remain at home pending a placement
hearing scheduled for March. I toed the line as best as I could
until the hearing.

I have mixed feelings about it all. It's true that I was out of
the control of my parents. Freedom was too enticing. But I felt
like an adult who should be allowed to live life as I chose. Coping
with me in those years would have been difficult for any parent. I seemed fine one moment and disappeared the next. Years
of heartbreak from Mikey had left my parents tired, depleted.
I thought that having me removed from the home might have
been a relief for them.

At the placement hearing, Dad agreed to bring me home
rather than letting the court send me to a group home. He
reminded me that I was home only because he had stood up for
me at the hearing. I felt a tinge of anger and thought to myself,
I'm your daughter; of course you should bring me home. On the day
Mikey was committed, might he have had a similar choice—to
stand up and say that she could come home? But he didn't. If my
parents' marriage had been intact, and Mom hadn't been seeing
Dave, would Mikey have been saved from the horror house that
was Camarillo? When I consider the possibility, it is difficult to
forgive them for letting Mikey go. But at the same time, was it
wrong for them to want to have a life?

truce

It was never articulated, but after the hearing there was an understood agreement between my parents and me: Don't run away. Stay in school. The implication was that if I met those requirements, I would be left alone.

Mom looked for more mainstream activities for me. In the late summer of 1970, the summer between tenth and eleventh grade, Anne and I went to a camp called an Encounter. She had not gotten into much trouble for running away. The National Council of Christians and Jews sponsored it, but there was nothing religious about the camp. There were about a hundred boys and girls, aged fifteen to eighteen. Issues of diversity, cooperation, personal growth, and creativity were all incorporated into the activities. At the same time, violence filled the streets of Los Angeles.

The camp was in a lush forest about ninety miles east of Los Angeles in the San Bernardino Mountains. We were surrounded by towering pines and slept in large cabins with wood floors and beams, covered by white canvas. Some of the kids straddled the line between troubled and mainstream, just like me. Most of the staff were laid back and cool.

I developed a romance with another camper. Peter was slight

and had thick dark hair and pale skin. He wore wire-rimmed glasses and looked like a bookish hippie. He was extremely soft-spoken and different from most of my other friends, with an interest in political science and philosophy. Peter was an avid reader like me, and we talked about Kahlil Gibran's *The Prophet* and Herman Hesse's *Siddhartha*. He was leaving for Brown University in Rhode Island shortly after camp ended.

Our physical relationship was limited to kissing, hugging, and holding hands. We liked each other a lot and agreed to try to keep up through letters and by spending time together when he came home for holidays and vacation. For a change, I looked forward to the start of school in the fall and to talking to Peter about my classes and books that I read.

We wrote for a couple of months, but he realized that he didn't want to commit to being exclusive with someone across the country. He said he'd had a life-changing experience on his first acid trip and was discovering a new world and meeting new people at college. I thought his honesty was honorable. I knew that he was fond of me and I understood his position. Disappointed, I accepted the break-up.

My optimism about school didn't last long. Many days began with Anne and me exchanging written fantasies, one- or two-page detailed descriptions of our dreams. We knew each other so well. Each fantasy was like a little present to the other. Our stories often spoke of days at Tree Park and of being swept up by someone we had a crush on. Reading them made first period more bearable.

It became increasingly difficult to attend class. We felt separate from our fellow students, even disdainful of them. We had experiences that they never would—running away, acid. They were straight, and we were little hippies. It didn't seem like the road I was traveling would ever intersect with theirs. I was more comfortable in and familiar with the world outside the mainstream. I would not be going to school football games, to the prom, or joining alumni groups after I graduated. *If* I graduated.

Santa Monica High School was an open campus, so it was

easy to leave unnoticed. There was a liberal dress code, and we wore hippie garb, quirky and colorful.

One day, Anne and I met each other in the corridor of the history building after first period. We grinned at each other and one of us said, "Let's go."

Walking briskly, we headed toward the Santa Monica Pier, five blocks away. But first we stopped at Sambo's Restaurant for a ten-cent bottomless cup of coffee. The cook sent us a free stack of buttermilk pancakes.

As we walked down the incline onto the pier, the brisk wind tousled our hair and painted the waves with white caps. The carousel was on our left. The intricately carved and painted horses were waiting quietly for the calliope music to begin. We passed the souvenir shop with its abalone shells, starfish, plastic trinkets, and postcards displayed in the large window. On weekdays, there weren't many people about, just a few solitary men with their fishing poles braced on the railing, lines in the water, bait boxes at their feet. After a half hour at the little coffee shop, we decided to walk to Tree Park. It was 11:00 A.M., and we had until 3:00 P.M., when school was over and we had to go home. Before leaving the pier, we stopped at the photo booth and sat for a couple of strips of black and whites, then sauntered along the ocean front headed south toward Venice. The beach was empty.

We passed Hot Dog on a Stick, the shabby hotel I had stayed at the first time I ran away, and Synanon, a famous drug rehab center housed in a once-elegant and exclusive beach club and spa. Synanon was mysterious because no one knew what went on inside.

We lingered on the boardwalk in Venice, hoping to see someone we knew, but it, too, was emptier now that the warm days of summer had passed. We spent most of the day trolling thrift shops on Main Street, looking for vintage velvet jackets or funky old shoes.

Anne spent the night at my house. Mom was at David's and Dad went to the Joker from 10:00 P.M. until closing time at 2:00 A.M.

As soon as he left, we took acid. The kitchen was dark, illu-minated only by the light on the stove. As we began to feel the acid, we switched on the overhead light and the room exploded in color. The yellow walls were a perfect canvas for multi-colored moving patterns. We sat at the kitchen table and talked all night, guffawing at something profoundly humorous or proclaiming our transient insights into the meaning of life.

Our voices became hoarse as the hours passed. When we got hungry, we munched on slices of buttered sourdough bread washed down with milk. We were so engaged in our conversation that we forgot that we were eating until I felt a lump of dough traveling down my throat and called out, "My bread's going down!" Then we burst out laughing until tears streamed down our cheeks. Dad stuck his head into the kitchen when he came home and we said hello, then goodnight, and he went to bed.

Toward the end of our trip, we went outside to watch the sunrise. The backyard was so neglected that it was filled with weeds. Some were three feet tall with sturdy stalks and yellow flowers—mustard weeds, my mother called them. We walked barefoot on the damp grass and stood under the pale sky. Glancing down at one of the plants, I noticed that slithering snails covered each stalk. I looked out over the expanse of the yard and saw that all of the plants were covered with them. The weed closest to me was waist high, and when I looked down again, the snails stretched their slimy necks and turned to look at me with their undulating antennae. "EEEWWW!" I called out. We turned toward the house and saw that there were dense patches of snails on the grass too. I don't know how this slipped our attention on the way out. We tried to pick our way through but crunched snails under our bare feet most of the way back to the house.

Our alliance deepened. I felt connected to Anne in a way I imagined sisters felt connected—like twins who don't always need to speak to understand each other.

hope

When I was sixteen, I wrote a poem about Mikey in my second-period English composition class. It was the only class I liked and often the only one I attended. Mr. Sawaya gave me an A. I wondered later if it was because he thought it was good or because he felt sorry for me.

MICHELE

aquarius born, you cannot see
you stopped speaking when you were three
the doctors said a damaged brain
at best they said you could be trained

mother and father did their best
year after year without any rest
good days bad days up all night
sometimes you'd scratch, sometimes you'd bite

but it took so little to bring you joy
you could sit for hours with the smallest toy
and when we turned the hi-fi on
you twirled around to your favorite song

in the family car you loved to ride
sometimes I wanted to run and hide
because the strangers always stared
you couldn't see them so you didn't care

one day you started to scream and yell
we thought it was pain but you couldn't tell
we rushed to the hospital right away
they committed you in a couple of days

camarillo was your new home
and you had to face it all alone
living among strangers who don't understand
what you want when you hold out your hand

when we went to visit you were covered with burns
the hostile patients must have taken turns
you must have been living in hell
but you couldn't speak so you couldn't tell

the nurses sit and gossip a lot
every once in a while they give you a shot
to knock you out so you're not in their way
five years now, day after day

after a visit, when we leave
you reach your arms through the bars and silently plead
we drive away, our eyes full of tears
each visit helps confirm our fears

I felt that, in spite of our unusual sibling relationship, I represented Mikey. She was my sister, after all. I still signed Mothers' Day and Christmas cards, "Love Mikey and Terry," just as I had always done.

Two months later, just after Mikey's eighteenth birthday, my mother finally won her long battle with the State of California to get Mikey transferred to Fairview Developmental Center. It was a spectacular victory. When the court committed Mikey to Camarillo, she was classified as mentally ill. The treatment was containment and major tranquilizers. It had taken a monumental effort to cut through the red tape to get Mikey reclassified as mentally retarded.

I wonder now if the judge at USC Hospital who committed her had just gotten it wrong. Did Mikey's violence lead to an incorrect diagnosis of mental illness? Or maybe violence was an automatic sentence to an institution like Camarillo. If the doctors had evaluated her correctly, would she have been sent to Pacific State or Fairview—facilities for the mentally retarded? She paid a terrible price for their decision.

Many years later, in 2013, the DSM V (the manual used for diagnosing mental disorders) was published. The broad category of "Neurodevelopmental Disorders" included "Intellectual Disability," previously called "Mental Retardation," and "Autism Spectrum Disorder." Mikey exhibited symptoms described in both disorders, but she was never diagnosed according to the newer criteria.

I think, too, that Camarillo administrators wanted Mikey out. Something catastrophic was bound to happen, and attentive family members made concealment difficult.

What mattered now was her safety. She would be with girls who had needs like hers.

Our family may have come apart when we lost the unifying purpose of caring for Mikey. But regardless of our circumstances at home, we still came together for her, and the day she moved to Fairview was a day to celebrate.

Mom, Dad, and I arrived at Camarillo at eleven in the morning. After signing Mikey out for the final time, we set out for the two-hour drive to Fairview—no county bus this time. As we drove away, I turned to look out the back window at the pastoral grounds that had seemed so deceptively tranquil and inviting five years ago. The mood was light, and I relaxed into my familiar role as the helper. Soft music played on the radio and Mikey rocked contentedly next to me on the back seat.

As we drove through the Fairview compound, I recalled our visit several years earlier when Mom and Dad rejected it. They couldn't have known the chain of events that would put her in Camarillo. Now we were exhilarated about her new home. We drove past the administration building and several cul-de-sacs of identical one-story beige buildings before arriving at Unit 27. Dad pushed the button on the wall near the locked door while Mom held Mikey's hand and spoke softly to her, telling her that she was a good girl. I carried a brown paper grocery bag full of new clothing, freshly labeled with an indelible marker, "Michele Sullivan—Unit 27."

The charge nurse greeted us warmly. She was expecting us. The first thing I noticed was that the furniture was pushed against the walls. Mikey would learn how to navigate here without always bumping into something. As one staff member took the bag of clothing, another came over to guide Mikey to a seat. Wisely, she found one slightly removed from the other girls. In this unfamiliar setting, it was striking to see how much institutionalization had changed Mikey. She was more docile, sort of robotic. Mom reassured her, telling her we would be back soon, and we began a tour of the unit.

As we walked down the corridor, I noticed posters of flowers tacked on the walls and some framed art. I felt a flash of annoyance. What's the point of art on the wall? The girls couldn't see it. As we continued, I saw more examples of efforts to create a homelike environment, pretty bedspreads and colorful pillows. After we left, I decided that even if the girls couldn't see the homey touches, they helped make the unit less barracks-like to staff and families.

We followed the nurse into one of the dormitories, and she showed us Mikey's bed. The little cabinet where her clothing would be kept already had her name written in black marker on white tape. We peeked into the dining room before entering a small conference room. The nurse informed us that they didn't use anti-psychotic medications on the unit because they weren't appropriate for this population. The doctor would review Mikey's records and make adjustments. We were relieved. Of course, her anti-convulsants would be continued.

Mom and Dad spoke about Mikey's explosions, explaining that too much sensory stimulation could precipitate an attack on herself or anyone nearby, but that attacks were often unpredictable. It was important to fully inform the staff. We knew that the residents here were more defenseless, more vulnerable to injury by Mikey. There were other residents who banged their heads and who had seizures. Some of them wore helmets. But there were no other biters. The nurse acknowledged my status as an honorary adult by asking me my thoughts. I suggested that they try feeding Mikey in a quiet setting, away from other girls.

She told us that the doctor, social worker, nurses, and dietician would evaluate Mikey. Then we would be invited to participate in developing her treatment plan. If there had been treatment-planning meetings at Camarillo, we were never invited.

Before we left the conference room, she handed Mom a yellow sheet of paper, a newsletter called Fairview Family and Friends. "I encourage you to get involved," she said, and explained that they hold regular meetings, plan events like holiday parties, and have a voice in policy decisions at Fairview. It all seemed like a dream—too good to be true.

Mikey stood up and reached out when she heard Mom and Dad's voices. We took her outside and sat together at a picnic table for a little while before returning her to the unit. Mom handed the nurse some Junior Mints to give to her as soon as we left to ease the transition. Mikey clung to Mom a little, but when the staff member guided her away, she went along without protesting.

I think we were afraid to be excited about Fairview. If we

wanted it too badly, it would be taken away, or once they learned how violent Mikey could be, they would punish her or send her back to Camarillo. We had plenty of experience at Camarillo hoping that people would be kind to Mikey, only to learn again and again that she was abused and neglected.

As we drove slowly toward the exit, Mom called out, "Look! Look at that!" I turned to look out the window and saw them, too—about fifty yards away, in a grassy area outside one of the units. "Oh my God, swings!" A snapshot memory flashed before me: Mikey in our backyard, a little girl swinging higher and higher, laughing out loud.

"Well, I'll be damned," Dad said as he pulled over so we could get out of the car to relish our discovery, a swing set with three dangling, unoccupied seats. Somehow—maybe it was because we could touch them—they made the possibilities of Fairview real. Surely, we were an exceptional family. How many can say that a simple, empty swing set could inspire so much hope? Hope that we had nearly lost.

We talked as we resumed our drive home, cautiously giddy about the kind nurse, the physical layout that was sensitive to the needs of the blind, about discontinuing medications that made her worse. They even have a dietician! Maybe they'll let Mikey eat with her fingers, strawberries and crackers with peanut butter on top.

mark

I turned seventeen shortly after Mikey was transferred to Fairview. I was in the eleventh grade. My probation ended, and the threat of foster care was lifted. I hadn't done a very good job of abiding by the rules, and I ditched more often than I attended class.

On the days that Anne and I weren't ditching school, we spent our time between classes and lunchtime loitering on 7th Street. It was quiet and little traveled, with a wide, grassy parkway that bordered the campus. Dozens of students sat on the parkway grass or the hoods of their cars to smoke, buy and sell drugs, and listen to music on the car radios. Kids who had dropped out or who attended Olympic Continuation High School also frequented 7th Street.

It's where I had been sitting a few months earlier when I learned that Jimi Hendrix had overdosed. A month later, Janis Joplin died. Those of us who were using drugs had espoused an old adage, made popular in the James Dean days: "Live hard, die young, and leave a beautiful corpse."

By now, I was not only taking LSD occasionally but selling it, too. As I sat on the grass with Anne one day at lunchtime,

Mark approached me. He'd dropped out of high school, but spent quite a bit of time at 7th Street. Anne was seeing his friend Larry.

The top several buttons on his patched shirt were unbuttoned, revealing a lot of curly, dark hair. He wore tight white jeans. I had noticed him before and found him very appealing.

The sun was in my eyes when I looked up at him. All I could see was a dark silhouette surrounded by bright light.

"Hi," he said in a distinctive, gravelly voice.

Shielding my eyes, I could see that he was smiling. His demeanor was relaxed. "Hi," I answered.

"I heard that you have some orange sunshine."

"Yeah, do you want some? A dollar each." His attention made me happy, nervous.

"Do you want to take some with us?" he asked.

I didn't know who "us" was, but I wanted to spend time with him. "Okay. When?"

"We could do it now."

"I don't think so. I wouldn't come down before I have to go home." I hoped that this wouldn't change his mind altogether.

"Okay," he hesitated. "Why don't you give me your phone number? I'll call you later."

He's the cutest guy around here, and he wants my phone number!

"Sure," I said. "EXbrook 91583."

"Thanks." He bought four tabs of acid, said "I'll call you later," then smiled and turned back to his friends.

Anne had been looking away, fiddling with a book, pretending not to be interested in my conversation with Mark. Now she faced me, and we put our heads together, laughing and celebrating my good fortune. There was potential here for us, once again, to have boyfriends that were also friends with each other. If I were involved with Mark, Anne and I would continue to do everything together.

He called me that night and invited Anne and me to come over to his house on Saturday. There would be other people there as well.

"Rick and I will pick you up at twelve. Bring some acid, too."

On Saturday, a silver Road Runner pulled up. Rick, Mark's stepbrother, was driving. He was a couple of years older than we were. Anne and I jumped in the back seat, and we sped off.

Mark lived north of Montana Avenue, in the most affluent part of town. There were about eight other people there, sitting on the back porch and in the sunny backyard. Some looked familiar and some I had never seen. Jimi Hendrix was turned up loud. Most of the day, a joint was being passed around, and several people took acid. I refrained on that day. I didn't want to repeat the experience of tripping around a bunch of strangers.

Mark and I, Anne and Larry, and various friends had time on our hands—no one went to school. Well, Anne and I went occasionally. Larry drove an old blue Ford Falcon and Rick his scary-fast silver Road Runner. When a car wasn't available, I took the bus to Mark's and, if it was late at night, took a cab home.

Rick's dad and Mark's mom had a life of their own and were content to leave the boys to themselves. We were young, free, and reckless. We took drugs, listened to music, and went to concerts at the Santa Monica Civic Auditorium. Mark, Rick, and others were shooting up cocaine and heroin. I was leery. I tried it once but didn't feel much. I was up to my knees in drugs, taking downers and psychedelics, but most of my friends were up to their necks.

My relationship with Mark resulted in my spending less and less time with my peace and music friends from Tree Park. It signaled a transition from a hippie mentality to a more superficial drug-based lifestyle.

My 1971 journal is both tedious and sad. I was preoccupied with Mark, and Mark was preoccupied with having sex with a lot of girls.

In October of that year, Mark and Rick were selling large quantities of cocaine. Unbeknownst to them, the police were monitoring the comings and goings at their house.

When they sold cocaine to an undercover policeman, they were arrested. Mark, a minor, was placed on probation. He stopped selling drugs out of his house, but otherwise his life-style was unaffected. Rick, over eighteen, faced a court hearing, and we waited to learn if he would have go to jail. Fortunately, I wasn't there on the day of the raid.

"call me father"

One day, after I had been seeing Mark for a few months, I asked him, "Would you like to come with me to visit my sister?" It was a test, and I knew he would fail it. I had told him a little about Mikey. He hemmed, hawed, and hesitated. "Welllll," he said, his eyes downcast. I didn't push. Yep, he failed my test. Mikey lived in a separate part of my life. She had been the most defining character in my family and my development, yet she would never be part of my normal life. I didn't have the will or confidence to expect someone to care enough about me to want to meet her.

Mom and Dad visited Mikey regularly, but I wasn't going as often. Weekends were my time to spend with Mark and friends. When I did go along, we did all of her favorite things: car rides, produce department visits, rides on the swings, and lots of yummy finger foods. Conflicts we may have been having at home disappeared when we were with Mikey. It didn't matter if we weren't speaking to each other or if we were arguing. Personal issues were put aside for Mikey.

She didn't become as agitated when we returned her to the unit at Fairview. The staff there was so much better handling her than the staff at Camarillo had been. The unit manager at Fairview called Mom regularly to tell her how Mikey was doing and how they were trying to cope with her aggressive outbursts, to identify what precipitated an explosion, and to protect Mikey and the other residents from harm. Sedating her was not an option.

I was familiar with the scenario of sitting quietly near Mikey when she reached out and grabbed hair, not letting go. But these girls were more defenseless than I. Here, Mikey was not the victim. I'm sure it was distressing to other parents when they learned that their child had been attacked.

Mikey was helmeted for a while to keep her from biting herself and others. The staff wrapped her wrists with bandages to try to protect her. The most effective intervention was what we had learned at home: remove her from others to a quiet place where obstacles are at a minimum, where she has enough room to spin and lash out. Provide her with a chair or bed for her to rest when the episode ended.

At home, reports from school showed that I ditched for weeks at a time and was failing most classes. I switched my major from English to art, thinking it would be easier to pass with minimum effort. I discovered that, unlike Anne, I was not artistically talented. We were still in the eleventh grade. When my parents set limits, I resisted them. My relationship with my mother and father became increasingly oppositional.

One day my mother, father, and I sat down in the living room to address my behavior. As a family, we had no experience resolving interpersonal conflict.

Dad turned his recliner toward me. I sat facing him on a chair on the other side of the room. Mom was on the couch between us. She was not emotive. Her usual calm self. But her tight-lipped scowl told me she was annoyed. Dad wanted to be a good father and do the right thing, but he was unequipped to respond to the difficult teenager that I had become. He'd been more or less dismissed by both my mother and myself. Where was the little girl who baked banana nut muffins and shared them with him while we watched *The Fugitive?* I had stopped calling him Dad and begun to call him Sully—not necessarily with the intent to disrespect, but because that's what everyone else called him and because I wanted to show that I was an adult. I didn't feel I should be subordinate to the adults in my life. I felt I should be treated like an equal.

When he tried to establish his authority that day in the living room, I argued and sulked, not giving an inch.

When he said, "I don't like your attitude, young lady," I glared at him, my arms crossed, and responded, "Well, I don't like yours, either."

Something snapped in him. He jumped so abruptly out of his chair that one of his loafers flew off his foot. He crossed the room in a couple of steps and, before I realized what was happening, grabbed my hair and began to hit me. His strikes must have been open-handed slaps—he didn't hurt me—but I was so startled and frightened by the out-of-control nature of his attack that I cried out, "I hate you! I hate you! I can't stand it when you touch me!" There was cruel venom to my outcry, an intent to wound.

He stopped. We all stood frozen for a moment. Mom seemed as stunned as I was, but also pained. She turned away from me and didn't say a word. Dad picked up his shoe, and after getting his jacket from his room he left the house.

Mikey was the only violent one in the family. The only time that I remember Mikey being hit was one night when she was about ten years old. She was awake all night. Dad wasn't getting any sleep at all. I heard his anger through the bedroom door as he yelled and hit her. I don't know how many times. I was afraid. I just lay there and listened. I left a note on Mom's pillow so she would see it when she came home, but she never said anything about it. He never hit me until that day. Mom had struck me a couple of times when I was very young. Her exasperation came to a boiling point once when I held my hands over my ears when she was speaking to me. Then there was that time when, at five or six, I had hidden in the garage. Anger had to percolate until it boiled over before it was ever expressed in our family, and it was frightening when it did.

Mom and Dad were so disconnected that there was no power in their approach to getting me in line. I exploited their lack of unity.

I don't know where Dad went after hitting me. He came home later that evening.

We didn't speak of our confrontation, but he told me a few days later, "From now on, you'll call me Father." I felt terrible about hurting him and, weeks later, told him that I was sorry. He didn't respond. I know the wound was deep.

Dad no longer traveled for work. He was in charge of a cable television company that served upscale Westlake Village, where he was well liked and respected.

It was only a couple of months later, in the fall of '71, that Dad's office manager found and furnished a nice one-bedroom apartment for him. It was close to work so he wouldn't have to drive forty-five minutes twice a day. Mom shopped for his dishes, linens, and household supplies. I don't recall a discussion about his plan to move or preparations for it.

On the day that he left, before he got into his car to drive away, he stood on the porch looking back into the living room at Mom. She faced him from a few feet away, drying her hands with a towel as though it was an ordinary day and she had just come from the kitchen. Her face was placid, impossible to read, yet I sensed impatience. I stood far across the room, an inconspicuous witness to what was happening. Dad's voice cracked when he said, "I never stopped loving you, Marcile." She was silent. A few seconds passed. *Would she say something kind?* I wondered. She was never one to say "I love you." Finally, she stepped forward and kissed him quickly, a peck, then stepped back. He turned and pulled the door closed. I think he was crying. I stood still, saddened by his pain but selfishly optimistic that my life at home would be less restricted.

My family had finally crumbled beyond repair.

Mom told me months later that my father was sure that when I ran away from home, I must have had to sleep with men to get by. That's why he washed his hands of me and moved out. It hurt to know what he thought about me, particularly because it wasn't true. Given the distance between him and my mother, once his relationship with me was broken, there was no reason for him to stay.

rick

Mom let Mark spend nights at our house. I don't think she particularly liked him, but she thought it was better to know where I was. I would have found ways to do what I wanted regardless. She had put me on the Pill, making her one of the cool moms. She didn't buy alcohol or allow drinking parties at our house. She didn't try to be one of us. But she bailed a couple of my friends out of jail.

Her boyfriend David sometimes acted like a surrogate father. He intimidated Mark with his Humphrey Bogart looks and his affiliation with bad guys in Gardena.

December 4, 1971. Mom was at Dave's. It was eleven o'clock at night, and Mark was staying at my house. We had turned off all the lights except for a soft amber light in my bedroom.

I had moved into Mikey's room. Dad had fixed the holes in the plaster long ago and painted the room a soft shade of peach. A floral rug covered the floor, and an antique silk sofa with a carved wood frame was placed in front of a window. My double bed was pushed into a corner and covered with a green madras bedspread. Matching curtains covered the windows.

Mark said he'd better call his mom and let her know he would be spending the night.

He listened quietly for a moment after she answered the phone.

"Were his sleeves rolled up?" he asked.

Another half hour passed, and the phone rang. It was Mark's mom. "Teresa, Richard's dead. Would you put Mark on the phone?" Her voice was flat and cold.

I dropped the receiver, speechless. He picked it up and, after a moment, hung up and said, "I've got to go home. Rick's dead."

"I know."

Rick was twenty-one years old.

We sat side by side on the edge of my bed. What could I say to comfort him? There must be a right thing to say, but I didn't know what it was, so I just waited silently with my hand on his thigh. After a few minutes, we turned on the lights in the living room to wait for my mom. I'd called her to drive Mark home.

The funeral was two days later. Mark was busy with his family; there were Jewish traditions to follow. I wanted to send flowers to the funeral home, but they were expensive. The florist suggested that "sometimes less is more," and I decided on a single long-stemmed red rose in a slender silver vase. I hand-carried it to the back door where flowers were delivered.

At the funeral, I wore a dark, knee-length purple dress and sat at the back of the synagogue with my mother. I could see that my rose had been placed prominently on a pedestal near the head of the coffin. It was as though the person who put it there knew that it was special. A gesture of love. I walked up the aisle, as did most other attendees, in single file, and looked at Rick in his coffin. The person lying there bore little resemblance to the boy I knew. His hair was slicked back away from his face. His lips matched the color of his skin, gray with a greenish cast. His hands were folded over his heart, and he was dressed in a suit he would never have worn. This was the Rick his father wanted him to be.

Mom and I left quietly after the ceremony and went home.

It was my first experience of the death of someone I knew. I thought of Rick as a big brother. I had cried on his shoulder with each of Mark's infidelities.

Mark and his friends continued to shoot up drugs as though nothing had happened. I was disgusted by it. "Don't you have any respect for Rick?" I demanded. I swore to myself that that one time I had tried IV cocaine would be my last. I would never put a needle in my arm again.

graduation

By January 1972, I'd gotten my GED. I turned eighteen in March and waited for Anne to turn eighteen in September. Then we would be able to move out of our parents' homes and move in together.

I had held part-time jobs intermittently since I was sixteen. My first job was at a retirement home, where I served dinner in the evenings and cleaned rooms on Saturday. Empty drinking glasses with dried Metamucil sat on side tables, and Jean Nate or Coty perfume scented the air. A nursing home was just across the courtyard, and it was always sad to see residents lose their independence when they were no longer able to care for themselves. After graduation, I worked at a trendy jean store called The Corral and learned that I was much more suited to caring for elderly people than I was to sales.

I moved into a small trailer in the backyard of Mom's house—the house where I grew up—and was free to do pretty much as I pleased. Her boyfriend David had his own apartment but spent most of his time at our house. Mom and I were getting along fine. Anne and I went on some little trips with Mom and Dave—Tijuana, Gilman Hot Springs where there was a small casino. I saw Dad when we went to visit Mikey. We all had our own lives now. The tension of my parents' unhappy marriage and my rebellious adolescence had dissipated once we were no longer under the same roof.

Anne and I continued to go to rock concerts—Linda Ronstadt, Rod Stewart—sometimes with our boyfriends, but often without. We drank wine out of a leather bota bag and danced in the orchestra pit or in the aisles. Again and again, we were bound together by the experiences we shared.

My unwillingness or inability to expect more from Mark hadn't changed. I went on (and on and on) in my diary about Mark and other girls, my disappointment in him, and my attempts to get closer to him. I thought that I would bring him closer if I didn't expect too much and if I acted as though I didn't need love and attention. It was what I had learned as a child, when not expecting too much made sense.

APRIL 24, 1972: Not much has changed inside me—I feel pretty much the same—alone.

When Anne turned eighteen in September, we applied for work at General Telephone in Santa Monica. I passed the qualification test with higher scores but, in order to stay with Anne, accepted a lesser position as a directory assistance operator. We worked the evening shift. GTE was in a tall art deco building on 7th Street. The entire twelfth floor was dedicated to operators and, when the elevator doors opened, a low buzz of voices filled the air. The operators' cubicles were open in a way that allowed the employees to speak quietly to each other during brief moments when they weren't on the line. We wore headphones with mouthpieces. I remember answering the click-sound, "Directory Assistance," and providing the requested telephone number. I can't imagine how we functioned without computers.

Anne and I rented a two-bedroom apartment in Santa Monica and furnished it with second-hand furniture. I loved the vintage vanity that I found for my bedroom. Anne sprinkled the entire apartment with patchouli oil. To this day, I am transported back to that living room when I smell patchouli. Our boyfriends sometimes spent the night—I was still seeing Mark. We worried that our neighbors would complain to our landlord.

I was happy. My life was my own. I had a boyfriend, a job, and an apartment with my best friend.

part three

Interlude

intensive care

I have no recollection of October 24, 1972, and only a few snap-shot memories from the following ten days. I learned what happened from Mom, bit by bit, over the next few weeks.

At about 10:00 P.M., she got a call from Santa Monica Hospital. An ambulance had brought me in with severe injuries. Luckily I carried a card in my wallet with information about who to call in an emergency. Mom left for the hospital immediately—it was only a few miles away. My father was in New York because of a death in his family.

When she arrived at the ER, a nurse informed Mom that I had been the passenger on a motorcycle that was hit by a car. Then she ushered her to a small room to wait for the doctor. Before the nurse left, she handed Mom a plastic bag that contained the bloody clothes that had been cut from me.

Dr. Duke Hanna, the neurosurgeon on call that night, entered the room and sat down facing my mother.

"Your daughter has been in a motorcycle accident," she remembers him saying. "She has a severe head injury and a broken leg. She might die. If she doesn't die, she might be a vegetable." He offered the news directly, without encouraging hope, perhaps to prepare her for the worst. I imagine that, at that moment, her calm matched his.

"Dr. Jones is her orthopedic doctor," he continued. "He'll be taking care of her leg, but we won't be doing anything about it now. We have to wait and see how she does. We're sending her up to ICU. You can wait with her in the emergency room until she is moved."

A nurse directed Mom to my gurney, parked against a wall in a brightly lit corridor. There were no wounds on my head, but my hair was matted with blood, and blood oozed from my ears. I clung to the side rails of the gurney, my eyes glassy, unrecognizing. As I attempted to raise myself, Mom supported my head, but a nurse rushing past said, "Lie down, honey." Just then I pulled myself up enough to lean over the rail and vomit a stomachfull of black blood onto the floor. I descended into a deep coma.

"Why is she in the corridor?" Mom demanded. "Why hasn't she been moved to intensive care?"

"We're waiting until midnight," the nurse said, explaining that my parents would be charged for a full day if they transferred me before midnight.

"No one asked you to save us money!" my mother remembers saying. When she told me this part of the story, I visualized her, fierce and protective. She was taking a stand for me, acting just as she had when her mother was burned and when Mikey was in the incubator.

Once I was transferred and a nurse had explained the visiting policies—ten minutes every hour—Mom called Aunt Phyllis and my father to tell them what had happened. Aunt Phyllis came to the hospital. Dad caught the first plane home.

Nearly two decades had passed since my parents sat vigil while Mikey was in the incubator struggling to survive. Now, once again helpless, they came together and did the same for me. Dr. Hanna told them that the first seventy-two hours were the most critical. If I didn't respond during that time, my chances of survival were slim.

I was lying down, and it was dark when I sensed Rick, Mark's stepbrother, at my side. It had been ten months since his death. I wasn't shocked or afraid. He didn't stay with me long, just long enough to reassure me that there was nothing to fear from what was going to happen next. Then I was no longer in a room or on a bed, but in another place surrounded by light yet also facing it—aware of a powerful presence, an entity. I was calm and unafraid. Curious. The presence asked me, "Do you want to stay or do you want to come with me?" The question didn't come to me in words, but I understood. At that moment, I knew that I stood at the threshold of another realm. I did not know what the world on the other side of the threshold was like, but I understood that the concerns, fears, and anguish of life did not exist there. Those things were part of living. I also knew that, while the presence would consider my wishes, the final decision was not mine. I paused. *I think I would like to stay but will gladly come if that is your decision.* There wasn't a specific reason I wanted to live; it just seemed that I wasn't finished. I sent my thoughts without words. There was a pause, then a response. It seemed like a nod, and it meant that I would be returning to my life. I was granted my return to this life without instruction, without a lesson plan—just to live.

I imagine that the light I experienced exists in a dimension, rather than in a distant place. A dimension that is invisible but all around me—a place that I will return to at the end of my life. Where I will meet the presence that spoke to me and loved ones who have passed before me.

While unconscious, I was enveloped in darkness, encased in ice blankets intended to reduce my brain swelling. Only my head and feet were exposed. Once, I heard my Aunt Phyllis's voice. She was speaking to my mother. "It seems that when your feet are warm, your whole body feels warmer." She was standing at the foot of my bed rubbing my feet vigorously, as my teeth chattered and I shivered violently. I couldn't open my eyes—couldn't speak to her to say, *"Yes, yes. Please don't stop."*

Mom said it was hard to watch when doctors and nurses measured the depth of my coma and judged the severity of brain damage. When I didn't respond to voices or touch, they looked for a response to pain by rubbing their knuckles on my sternum and watching my face for a reaction. A response to pain was a good sign. One nurse showed Mom a different way to check by grabbing my nipple and pulling and twisting hard. Mom could tell that this was a particularly painful test because of the way my face contorted. It was good news that I reacted, but Mom didn't like that nurse.

At one point I caught a glimpse of a monitor at the side of my bed. I must have been semi-conscious then. I knew that the green light blipping across the screen meant my heart was beating, and I was glad.

I'm not sure if they kept the lights low in the ICU—my memories are dim and blurred. I called a nurse a cunt when she gave me a painful injection in my butt. That was a good sign that I was regaining consciousness. "Don't call me any of your filthy family names," she said, and slapped me. I learned later that patients with head injuries often spew profanity.

One day, I heard Mom ask me, "Do you know who this is?" I fought up from the darkness. It was hard to open my eyes. A face came into focus—my childhood pediatrician. He was looking at me kindly with a warm smile, and his presence comforted me. He was a gentle man, with cool hands and a cold stethoscope. When I saw him as a child, his plump, middle-aged nurse always rewarded me with a lollipop when she gave me a shot. "Dr. Ireland," I said weakly before returning to the darkness.

in the hospital

My earliest memories after the accident, after I was transferred from ICU to a regular hospital room, are jumbled. In and out of consciousness, I don't know in what order they occurred. People came to visit, I closed my eyes, and when I opened them again, they were gone. I didn't know if minutes or days had passed.

One day I awoke and didn't have any idea where I was. The white sheets were rumpled; there were raised rails on each side of the bed, and the head of the mattress was slightly elevated. Natural light filled the room. My left arm lay relaxed at my side. I was staring at my palm, dark purple, badly bruised. I was confused, and couldn't take my eyes away. I didn't realize Mom was sitting in a chair beside me until she spoke. "You and Anne were in an accident on your way home from work. You're in the hospital." I wasn't conscious enough to assimilate much more information, but I asked her, "Where is Anne?"

"She is at home. She wasn't hurt as badly as you were." I slipped back into semi-consciousness.

I asked the same questions over and over—sometimes because I forgot the answer and sometimes because I wanted to hear what happened to me again and again. I was like a little girl asking for a bedtime story.

Another day, I opened my eyes and saw my father sitting next to my bed. "Daddy."

Once I opened my eyes to blurry red shapes close to my face. Then, through the blur, I saw my cousin John smiling at me. It had taken a moment before I realized that he was holding out a bouquet of red roses. "Johnny," I said, relieved to find my footing in reality. When the flowers were set aside, I saw that my aunt and parents were also there, standing beside or at the foot of my bed. Then I slipped back to sleep.

It was late at night when I woke up and had to pee. The room was quiet and dark, but the light from the corridor illuminated the edges around the doorway. I climbed out of bed, which wasn't easy because the side rails were up and I had a full leg cast on my left leg. After taking a couple steps, I felt myself falling. My broken leg had not yet been set, and my intact leg could not hold me up.

I grabbed onto the side of the doorway and yelled, "Help," as I slid down toward the floor. People came running, and, one on each side of me, they lifted me off the ground. "Please put me on the toilet. Please," I begged. No such luck. They picked me up and put me on a bedpan.

I must have let out a torrent of profanity; the patient who shared my double room told my mother she had never heard anything like it. Before the nurse left the room, she put a vest on me that tied to the bed rails and kept me from getting out of bed.

I was in a private room after that, and Mom stayed most of the time. Dad was there every day as soon as he could get away from work. I was afraid that I would wake up at night, confused again, and fall when I tried to get out of bed. So I asked for the restraint vest. It made me feel safer.

There was a parade of doctors every day. Dr. Hanna, the neurosurgeon, asked me, "Do you know your name?"

"Teresa Sullivan."

"Do you know where you are?"

"The hospital."

"Do you know why you are here?"

"I was in an accident."

"Do you know what day it is?"

"No."

"Smile."

I did.

When Dr. Jones, the orthopedic surgeon, visited, he touched my toes and said, "Wiggle your toes."

I did.

He smiled, and the skin around his eyes crinkled. I thought he seemed satisfied.

Finally, he told my Mom they were ready to set my leg.

I heard him tell her a story about the Civil War. Men injured in battle often had to wait days before broken bones could be set, and doctors had learned that even with long delays, limbs could be saved.

I'm not sure if it was before or after my leg was set that Dr. Jones came into the room with a white plastic apparatus. It was a saw with a spinning circular blade. He was going to cut a window into my cast so he could observe the wound where my bone had protruded. I screamed and screamed for him to stay away from me. Sobbing, I clutched the side rails on the bed and looked to my parents for help.

Mom told me later that she had an idea of why I was so afraid. The ambulance driver had told her that when he found me on the pavement my leg was in the air bending up and down at the knee. Most likely as I lay on my back flapping my leg, I had seen only the bone that protruded, and Mom thought I might wonder if my leg was gone. She and my dad lifted both legs, the left one in a heavy cast, the right one bare. They wanted me to see both of my feet. They moved each toe, and as they did, I stopped crying and grew calm. They promised me that my leg would be okay and held my hands as the doctor cut a 3 x 3-inch square in the cast.

I was beginning to be aware for longer periods of time. Sometimes I knew the difference between yesterday and today, but I still lapsed into sleep or unconsciousness without warning. I still woke up and stared at the bruises on my left hand. My mother explained again that I had been on the back of a small motorcycle, more like a large scooter, that Anne had borrowed from her boyfriend Keith. We were on our way home from work. As we drove through an intersection two blocks from home, we were broadsided by a sports car making a left turn. Anne's leg had been broken and set. She was no longer in the hospital. She hadn't come to see me.

Mom explained that I had head injuries. My skull was fractured, and I had bled into my brain.

Brain damaged? I was brain damaged, I thought to myself. I knew what that meant.

Filled with terror, I asked my mom if she was going to send me away.

She reassured me, "No, no." But the fear remained.

Late at night, when my room was dark and quiet, I wondered if I had made the right choice. I was afraid—afraid of being so damaged that I would forever be separate from others. I considered hitting my head against something and starting the hemorrhage again, but I also knew it was too late to choose to die, to be with the light in that other place. The opportunity had passed. I had made my choice.

Another doctor, Dr. Strand, smiled and winked at me when he entered my room.

I smiled back. He came closer, his face only a foot from mine.

"Smile." "Close your eyes." "Wink." He demonstrated each movement.

I complied with his instructions.

I thought he was just particularly friendly, but Mom explained that the left side of my face was paralyzed. It didn't feel paralyzed.

Then, two weeks into my hospitalization, I looked at myself

in a mirror. I thought I looked pretty good, like myself. I had anticipated seeing my head swathed in bandages. There was only a bruise on my forehead. I tried smiling and winking. The right side smiled, but the left side just stared back at me. I squeezed my eyes shut, but only one closed.

For some reason, this didn't distress me. Perhaps the head injury had blunted my responses, but I came to believe that my calm was a gift I had received when I chose to return to life—a gift of acceptance that would help me through the next year.

When I tried to pour water from my pitcher into a cup, I repeatedly missed and spilled it all over my bed. An ophthalmologist determined that I saw double because there was damage to a nerve that allowed movement in my eye. It explained why it was almost impossible to manage using crutches when going up or down steps.

Only time would tell if the nerve in my face would recover. There was some discussion of stitching my left eye shut so it wouldn't dry out. I slept with a damp washcloth over my eyes.

I told my mother about my meeting with Rick and the light. For more than a decade I didn't speak of it to anyone else, for two reasons: it was exquisitely personal, and I thought perhaps it wasn't supposed to be shared. Also, I was afraid that people would think I was crazy or dismiss me as brain-damaged.

The ambulance drivers came to visit me. They told me that people sitting in a restaurant on the corner of the intersection told them that they had heard a scream. Neither Anne nor the car driver saw the accident coming. Someone from the restaurant probably called the ambulance. They found me on the ground thirty feet from the accident.

Mark visited. Family and friends. I had flowers and get-well cards in abundance. Relatives in Illinois had prayers said for me at their churches. Anne didn't call or come to see me. I wasn't angry but perhaps confused. I didn't call her, either. I'm not sure why. I didn't call anybody. I was still in and out of a dreamlike state.

One friend asked if I wanted him to bring me some Angel

Dust. It took me a moment to realize what he was saying. I never wanted to be out of touch with reality again. PCP was the last thing I wanted. It was my first inkling that I might not fit in with my friends anymore.

Shortly before the end of my hospital stay, on one of Dr. Strand's visits, he saw a tiny muscle under my eye move. He was like a little kid on Christmas who got a present. He gathered the other doctors and my family around my bed to show me off and explained that the movement meant that the nerve had not been severed—that I might recover more movement. I began to practice, in front of a mirror, moving that tiny little muscle. It was a good omen.

Finally, after three weeks and three days, I was discharged. Two of my favorite nurses took the time to wheel me personally out to Dad's car. They hugged me and wished me luck.

recovery and
a trip to europe

moved into the middle room of Mom's house—the house I had grown up in. It had a small bathroom and easy access to the kitchen.

Shortly after I returned, Anne came to visit. It was evening when she arrived, dark outside. She was wearing a long-sleeved t-shirt and an ankle-length skirt that concealed her cast. Crutches were the only indication that she had been hurt, and she navigated easily with them. Our exchange felt awkward, our conversation superficial. I didn't ask why she hadn't visited me in the hospital. When I had asked others, they said, "Maybe she feels guilty." I assumed they meant for the accident. But I didn't hold her responsible.

"My dad moved my stuff out of the apartment," she said.

"Mine too," I replied. My antique dresser that was just like Anne's was against a wall across the room, but the large round mirror that was part of it had been broken during the move.

Anne had moved back home with her dad. Even though

she continued to work at the telephone company, she wouldn't be able to afford the apartment alone.

"What did the landlord say?" I asked.

"He was okay."

"How's Keith?" I asked. It was small talk.

"He's okay. Pissed off about his motorcycle."

After about fifteen minutes, Mark arrived to visit. As soon as he came into the room, Anne stood up, got her crutches in position, and said, "Well, I have to go now." She said "Hi" to Mark as she passed him on her way out.

As soon as she was gone and Mark was sitting down, I looked him in the eyes and said, "You know, I wish I had learned it from you instead of Anne." He broke eye contact, fidgeted, and mumbled a feeble excuse. They'd had sex while I was in the hospital.

I'm not sure which betrayal hurt most. Anne's, I think. I was accustomed to Mark's infidelities. In a way, it was a relief. It made it easier to distance myself from my friends now, rather than feel the sting of not fitting in later. I knew that while my friends wouldn't necessarily dump me, their lives would continue as before and I'd no longer fit in. I didn't want to. I didn't want to take drugs, I needed help getting around, I wasn't as pretty, and I was too serious—not as much fun.

A week after I returned home from the hospital, I received a letter from my social worker, Mrs. Eberhardt:

Hi dear one,

It was good to talk to you yesterday—and I hope we get to talk in person before too long. I sensed that the horrible accident may have tripped off quite a spiritual-type of reaction also . . .

Certainly being so near death and now still "being" is an experience not too many of us encounter.

But all changes within ourselves also affect the other important people in our lives—some can come along with our change, understand them & that is

good—some cannot and that is sad even if we must
accept that also. Only time—certainly not worry—can
tell us the answers.

There is a separate world where people with serious illness and disability spend time. Growing up with Mikey had made me familiar with it. We see each other in doctors' waiting rooms and hospital corridors. Some of our disabilities are visible—casts or a paralyzed face. Sometimes we look perfectly normal. Some disabilities will last a lifetime, some won't. Unlike outsiders, we don't stare at each other but neither do we look uncomfortably away. We have a kinship and acknowledge it with a smile or nod. Sometimes, without prying, we ask a question.

After the accident, when I was out in public, at a restaurant or store, people stared at me. Sometimes I was in a wheelchair because it was easier than crutches, especially if there were stairs. I was fitted with a contraption like a pair of glasses that used prisms to help move my eye into place. They worked fairly well when I looked straight ahead, merging the two images together when I watched TV but weren't helpful when I looked down. Paralysis distorted my facial expressions. Again, growing up with Mikey made me familiar with the stares of strangers. I didn't like it, but I tried to be nice. More often than not, people asked me if I had injured myself in a skiing accident. "No. It was a motorcycle accident." Sometimes I thought I saw a flash of disdain, so eventually I just told them that, yes, it was a skiing accident.

I knew I was fortunate, that I could have died, or I could have been as brain-damaged as Mikey. But it was the effect of my near-death experience that smoothed a path for me. I felt an equanimity that was striking in light of the difficulties I faced.

Medical tests and procedures colored the next six months. Electroencephalograms—pins in my scalp to evaluate brain damage; electromyograms—pins in my face to evaluate muscle function; exams to assess my eye muscles. X-rays of my leg revealed that the bones weren't healing in proper alignment, but bowing outward. My orthopedic surgeon made several measurements and cut wedges in each side of my cast. Then, using one hand near my ankle, below the wedges, and one hand above the wedges, he pulled in opposing directions, using the plaster to move the bones. Dr. Jones had warned me that it would hurt, but there isn't a good way to prepare for pain, especially when you don't know how bad it is going to be. As he moved my bones, a whimper escaped my lips before I could contain it. I clenched my teeth and clutched the gurney rails beneath me until my knuckles turned white. At least I knew what to expect when he had to repeat the procedure, three times over the next few months.

I had a square blue plastic cube, about five inches on a side, that contained batteries. Two covered wires protruded from the box, and there was a quarter-sized metal circle on the end of each. Three times a day, I soaked two small pieces of paper towel with salt water (a good conductor). Then I placed an electrode on top of the wet paper towel in front of my left ear, where the nerve emerged, and the other electrode above my left eyebrow. When I pushed a button on the box, an electrical volt surged into my face, contracting the muscle—my eyebrow shot up. The shocks were painful, especially on my forehead, but not unbearable. I saw a white flash with each one. After ten shocks, I moved to a different muscle. My lips moved up into an involuntary left-sided smile. Ten more shocks, then one more section. The doctors hoped that by forcing my muscles to contract, I would be spared a permanently drooping face due to atrophy. Only time would tell how much function would return.

My parents gave me time, attention, and support. I didn't feel guilty about it. Mikey was safer now, and it was okay to be the center of attention because I was badly hurt and I needed help. Mom had broken up with Dave just before the accident, so Dad spent a lot of time with us. I loved being with them.

Mom and I played gin rummy and Boggle. I learned to play poker so I could join in the family games with Mom, Aunt Phyllis, and my cousins. Mom, Dad, and I went out for dinner and, of course, there were the doctor visits. Often, in the following years, Dad told me how much he admired my fighting spirit. "You were knocked down and got up fighting. You never quit." It felt good to know he was proud of me. I had learned calm in the face of adversity from the day I was born. My parents modeled putting one foot in front of the other. Tenacity and perseverance served me well.

My face and vision gradually improved. After seven months of taking sponge baths, my cast was removed. I had been excited about the prospect of sitting in a bathtub, but it was an entirely disappointing experience. It was difficult getting into the tub with my shriveled leg, and then sitting on the hard porcelain in cooling water. It took a little longer for the muscles in my leg to become strong again.

When I could finally walk with confidence, in the summer, Mom, Aunt Phyllis, cousin John, cousin Cathy, and I decided to take a trip to Europe. And what a trip it was! We bought a used Volkswagen van in front of the American Express office in Amsterdam. We prepared our "home" by making red, white, and blue curtains for all the windows, and by purchasing blankets, dishes, and a small stove. After a few days in Amsterdam, we set out for our six-week trip. We had a general plan about where we wanted to go and things we wanted to see, but if we saw a road that intrigued us, we took it. If we wanted to stay somewhere a few more days, we stayed.

John did most of the driving and slept on the bench seat up front. After folding the back seat down at night, we four women slept like sardines. When one turned, the others had to shift to accommodate. Every few days we stayed at an inexpensive hotel so we could shower. There were public bathhouses in Germany, so we didn't need to spend money on hotel rooms there.

I limped through cobblestone cities hundreds of years old and toured Hitler's concentration camp in Dachau. I watched tanks rolling through the streets of Yugoslavia, apparently a routine occurrence in the communist country and so very, very different from home. Mom and I split up from the rest and took the night train, the Lusitania Express, from Madrid to Lisbon. Our relationship was easy and relaxed. We had fun together as we visited the Alfama district in Lisbon and listened to Fado music. I still get tears in my eyes when I hear the mournful refrains. By the time we came home, we had visited nine countries. I was enthralled by Europe. The experience of feeling so small in the face of such history and different cultures put life in perspective.

picnic

*DECEMBER 11, 1973: Been a long time since I wrote.
I don't feel I can adequately explain what's happened
in my life during the past year, but it's been the most
important year in my life.*

*Although I sometimes get very lonely (I haven't
really established much social life since my break with my
old life) I don't take dope anymore. I've never been closer
to my mother and my father, but especially to my mom.*

*I registered in school in English, sociology, and
psychology. I'm crazy about psychology. My Dad is
helping support me while I'm in school.*

*Basically, this has been the best year of my life,
and I think it will have a very strong and good effect
on every year to come.*

While I was learning about behavior modification in my
psychology classes at Santa Monica City College, Fairview was
practicing it on Mikey. Reward and punishment were used to
change unwanted behaviors. When she bit herself, the staff put
a paper bag over her head. It didn't help. Maybe it would have

worked better for a sighted person. But she was doing well in many ways. It was 1974, and she had been institutionalized for nine years.

For six months she was paired with a student named Shelly from the local college. Shelly was enrolled in a two-year program to become a licensed psychiatric technician. She was excited about her work and motivated to try to improve the quality of life for someone like Mikey. She brought toys that challenged Mikey. Sometimes she took her to the pool on the grounds and Mikey got to splash in the shallow end. We were sad when Shelly's internship ended.

Back in the fold of the family, I began to visit Mikey more often. On weekends, Dad drove forty-five minutes to pick Mom and me up. Then we made the hour-long trip to Fairview.

On one visit, I stood nearby while Dad pushed Mikey on a swing; I was surprised by an unwelcome twinge of anger. Not toward Mikey. But catastrophe, in the form of my accident, had brought me the time and loving attention from my parents that had been scarce when I was a child. I felt angry with them for not finding a way to make more room for me and for not protecting me from Mikey's violence. I knew my feelings were immature and unacceptable, so I pushed them aside and took my turn pushing Mikey on the swing.

Decades later, I discovered a memoir called *Boy Alone*. The author, Karl Greenfield, told his story about growing up with Noah, his autistic younger brother. Many years earlier, my mother had read the book written by Noah's father, in which he spoke about his anguish over institutionalizing Noah. As I read, Karl's words touched the sadness and isolation that I had known. *"I am learning that I can never compete with you. I will lose every race for our parents' time and attention."*

Eventually, I understood that unacknowledged pain congeals into anger. I had to feel the sadness, had to scrape away the scab before I could heal.

Fairview Families and Friends held an annual picnic for

residents and families. It was quite an extravagant production, with live music, food, and trolley rides. The picnic I remember most vividly happened on a beautiful summer day. There were dozens of residents of all ages, some blind, some in wheelchairs, all of them developmentally disabled. Some were in groups accompanied by Fairview staff. Some were lucky to have family members. We brought a large blanket and spread it out close to where a band played rock and roll. The Markeson family was sitting not far away. Mr. and Mrs. Markeson were perhaps the most active parents in Fairview Family and Friends. Every weekend, they visited their daughter Karn, who was on Mikey's unit and who was sometimes violent, too. They worried about what would happen to Karn when they passed away. All the parents, particularly the ones with the most profoundly handicapped children, lived with uncertainty about the future.

Mikey was enjoying hot dogs and ice cream, seeming to sense the happy vibe of the day. The music was loud. She stood, and I did, too, to accompany her through the maze of blankets and people. "Where are we going, Mikey?" She pulled me toward one of the four-foot-tall speakers near the stage. She could feel the bass beat reverberating through the air. As soon as she touched the speaker, she sat and placed her hand against it. For the next hour, she sat, rocking gently, with a grin on her face.

Being with Mikey reminded me of what was important in life, and what was superficial and selfish.

hole in my head

My fear of brain damage resulting from the accident didn't go away. I wondered if my parents asked teachers, or paid them, to give me good grades so that I wouldn't know how different I was from normal people. I thought the teachers felt sorry for me.

There was a new, cutting edge test called a CAT scan. It allowed Dr. Hanna to see more clearly just how much brain damage I had. After the test, I walked into his office and said, "I'm doing really well in school—all As."

He smiled and said, with his blunt humor, "That shows just how much you can do with a hole in your head."

He showed me the picture of the abnormality in my CAT scan. There was a white area on the right side of my brain about the size of a quarter. He explained that, when the brain tissue was damaged, it left a hole that filled with fluid—a "post-traumatic cerebral cyst," he called it. Seeing the image didn't slow me down. It only reinforced my resolve to work hard.

It was 1974 and I was twenty years old. Mikey was in a better place, and I had begun a new life. I would like to say that I had finally and permanently joined the world that I once thought of as normal. I was a normal person. And I wanted to be. I was doing normal things, traveling, and going to college. No more drugs. No more empty relationships.

But it wasn't that simple.

part four

Passages

double life

strived to achieve and to earn the approval and self-esteem I craved. I wanted to live up to my potential and compensate for my failures. But for the next seven years, I straddled a line. Back and forth between two worlds, never quite fitting into either.

MAY, 1974: Still going to school—tho not doing as well—combination of classes not as inspiring and I'm spending nearly all of my time w/Erny. Oh yes, I'm seeing someone from the same group of people that I was so proud of myself for leaving. Erny's 27 and going to school too. We have many interests in common (primarily scholastic) but we reinforce each other's laziness (at least mine), and I find myself sloughing off in my studies. I guess I'm in it basically because of my need for some emotional security in my life—more than a family can provide—but I'm realizing that there is no security in our relationship.

The primary factor that keeps us seeing each other is sex and companionship though the companionship leaves a lot to be desired.

*Find myself disliking myself for getting involved
w/Erny and setting similar pattern as in the past but it's
always hard to break the pattern and just as hard to just
back away. Still don't take dope anymore. I get scared
sometimes when I get pains in my head. Don't want
to waste my life. I've spent too much time in the past
doing that*

Once I started spending time with Erny, it was inevitable that my path would cross Anne's. In late summer 1974, on a warm and sunny day, she and I were driving in Santa Monica. I was at the wheel of Mom's gray Datsun. I didn't give much thought to the hurt of the past. Anne and I never discussed it. I didn't think, *should I or shouldn't I?* before I decided to move into an apartment with her again. Not even a coin toss. Once again, I was at an intersection but didn't see the signs.

As we drove, David Bowie's song "Fame" came on the radio. How can I explain what happened next? We began to sing, rocking to the music, just as we had at many concerts over the years. The music and Anne's company transported me to the happy, good old days. We were two blocks from the beach when we drove past an apartment building. The lower apartment, facing the street, had lots of windows, in one of which a "For Rent" sign was propped. The address for the property manager was just a block away.

"Let's go," Anne said.

"Okay."

Thirty minutes later, we were the new tenants.

*SEPTEMBER 16, 1975: Must say I've been living a
different life here than at Mother's house. Maybe I've
been living too hard & loose the past week or so but I'm
sort of celebrating my new independence, and soon I'll
have to settle down and go to work. Been drinking a
lot. Staying up all night. We've had a lot of people here.
I got a job as a waitress.*

OCTOBER 10, 1975: It seems I keep getting myself
into unhappy situations—feeling wasteful of myself,
lost, alone. The old pattern returned tonight. I wanted
just to take a pill or get drunk and escape it all.

Whenever I drank, I drank until I was so intoxicated that I often didn't remember what happened. The house was full of people most of the time—many of them shooting heroin. I threw out syringes that I found lying on the sink in the bathroom and kicked people out of the house at two o'clock in the morning. If I hadn't been paying part of the rent, I imagine I'm the one who would have been kicked out. I was taking Percodan and Valium but continued to keep my promise to myself never to use a needle.

When I reconnected with Anne and we moved into our apartment, I had hoped for the same things I had hoped for before our accident: living with my best friend, having a job, and living a normal life. We would still have fun—concerts, some drinking, boyfriends—but our lifestyle wouldn't be destructive. Instead, each night our home was full of people that I didn't know and more drugs. I participated, but maintained some separateness for the sake of self-preservation.

Two months after moving in, I escaped to Houston to find a better life with a man named Roger. Initially brought there by a friend of his, he had been spending time at our apartment because our place is where the heroin was. Roger was a Vietnam vet, addicted, quiet, and withdrawn. He wanted to get clean, get a job, and live a normal life. We wanted a fresh start. Once in Houston, I was unable to get into a nursing training program and could only find work as a cocktail waitress. That, coupled with Roger's emotional withdrawal, meant that after three months, I returned to Santa Monica.

Over and over, my loneliness led me back to Anne. The promise of the sisterly connection we had known in the days when we shared everything was still a lure, even though the carefree days were over. In spite of my past experiences, Anne and I moved, with our boyfriends, into different apartments in the same complex. Drugs, alcohol, overdoses, suicide, and even murder colored our world, which became increasingly dark and dangerous. It scared me. Really scared me. I didn't want to live this life. I knew that I had to break all ties.

When I left old friends behind, particularly Anne, it wasn't because I thought I was better than them or because I thought they would pursue me and entice me into using. I knew, deep in my bones, that I would drown in drugs if I stayed. My decision to never use a needle wasn't entirely because of Rick's death. The needle represented the last rung of a ladder descending into a place from which I would never emerge.

So, once again, I grasped at a chance for a better life. My relationship with my mother was strained, but she had been looking for a way to help me and found a federally funded program for vocational nursing. I applied and was accepted.

In June 1976, I started school. Then I kept going.

JULY 18, 1979: First entry in years! Graduated from SMC with Associate Degree in Registered Nursing last month. On the dean's list every semester. Took state boards—HARD! Will begin work at UCLA on August sixth. Made a few friends and lost/left a few over the years. My best friend now is Maxi my dog—a real sweetheart. I won a meager settlement from the accident of 10/24/72. Essentially broke now but my living expenses low here. Dad's in Westlake still working at "Conejo Cable" and unhappy—must be lonesome— what a sad situation. Mom unhappy too—if you ask me.

New life ahead—a little scary, but optimistic— much more positive than past. Worked hard past three years. I'm smarter than I thought and stronger.

I was at ease professionally; felt equal to doctors and to fellow nurses; was confident and calm in a crisis. Well, people thought I was calm. I had learned through a lifetime to approach crisis matter-of-factly. Others turned to me to take charge. But socially I wasn't confident. I still felt different. In spite of my outward success, I feared that those around me would discover that I wasn't one of them. Failed attempts at relationships were painful. I confused yearning with love.

One night at work, the nurse from the day shift informed me that the mother of one of our patients was staying at his bedside. The patient, a young man in his twenties, was blind, brain-damaged, and didn't speak. His mother was there to comfort him if he awoke and to help keep him in bed so that restraints wouldn't be necessary. I made rounds, as I always did at the beginning of my shift, walking into the dimly lit rooms, looking at each patient. I checked to see if their IVs were dripping on time and if the prior shift had completed vital signs checks (temperature, pulse, blood pressure, and respirations). I verified that fluid intake and urine output had been tallied. I took a pulse, felt the temperature of the patients' skin, looked at dressings and wounds. I asked if they were in pain. Most of the patients were sleeping that night. As I worked my way up the corridor, I entered the room where a middle-aged woman was sitting at the side of the bed where her son slept. I approached her, and after inquiring about how she and her son were doing, I asked her gently if he had been born prematurely. His severe impairments were identical to Mikey's. I supposed that her life had been and was still consumed with caring for him. "No," she answered, "a motorcycle accident."

"Oh," I replied. "I'm sorry." I told her that I would be checking on him throughout the night and to let me know if she needed a break. I continued my rounds, pausing in the corridor for a moment. I had been startled by her response. It had been a while since I had been reminded of my own miracle—my gift of life, my reprieve from a life like Mikey's.

My shift ended at 9:30 A.M. I went home and followed my usual morning ritual: Take my dachshund Maxi out to pee, feed her, spread newspapers in the windows to make the room dark, put in earplugs, warm up a half-cup of milk, add a half-cup of Southern Comfort, strip, get into bed by 11:00 A.M. and hope for sleep. At 7:00 P.M. I'd get up to start my workday over again. I had every other weekend off and sometimes went with Mom and Dad to see Mikey.

Throughout school I'd stayed completely away from Anne and old friends. I'd continued to drink but was able to restrict it to weekends.

In 1980, a year after beginning work at UCLA, I went to a Christmas party attended by doctors and nurses I knew. The following day, when I came to work, I apologized for the night before. I remembered arriving at the party but nothing after that—because I was too drunk. It hadn't been my intention to get wasted. In spite of my history, I couldn't see that once I started drinking I wouldn't be able to stop. I apologized to my co-workers preemptively because I was certain that I had drawn attention to myself in an unflattering way. I was embarrassed and decided that I shouldn't socialize with co-workers.

FEBRUARY 9, 1980: I still feel like I'm not making it in the world I want to be part of, and I'm not sure I am up to trying.

Old friends resurfaced, and—surprise—I began spending time with Anne again. Maybe this time it would be different, I thought, deluding myself. In no time at all, Anne and I were doing what we always did: drinking, using, and getting involved with losers. Once again, I was pedaling backwards from all I'd achieved.

One night in February 1981, we ran into Warren at a bar. He had been a frequent visitor to 2nd Street in the days before I had pulled my life together.

Warren and I began spending time together and, during an afternoon at my place, I offered him some cocaine. I knew in my heart that this was another man more interested in my drugs than in me—a familiar scenario. "If I'm going to do coke," he said, "I'm going to do it the right way." It only took a minute to break the promise that I had made to myself ten years earlier. Warren had a syringe with him and injected both of us.

My downward spiral was at warp speed. I descended into despair and self-hatred. I seldom worked, knowing that I was jeopardizing my job. I challenged myself: *What's wrong with you? How could you wreck your life like this? You've been witness to such misfortune and you were spared. You had every opportunity and you threw it away. How could you be so selfish and cavalier with the life you were given—the life that you yourself requested?*

Within a year, I was drowning in cocaine and heroin. I couldn't find the bridge between worlds. I had tried desperately to honor the gift of life I was granted after my motorcycle accident, and I felt ashamed that I had failed so completely.

In that transitional window between life and death eight years earlier, I'd understood that the trials of my life were temporary. But in the emptiness my life had since become, I'd distorted the message. I had twisted it to believe that nothing in this life mattered. Nothing.

My mother discovered that I was using intravenous drugs one day when she stopped by my house and, finding a mess, emptied a trashcan and discovered dozens of syringes. She confronted me, more concerned than angry or judgmental. I told her that I was going to stop. I know she wanted to believe me. I didn't tell her that I had been trying desperately to stop for months and had failed over and over. I tried to maintain a thread of connection to family, Mom, Dad, and Mikey. Tried to maintain a scrap of a normal life.

I had been in the emergency room twice, once after being assaulted by someone I used with, and once for an infection from shooting up in my foot. Finally, I gave up—stopped trying to stop. I seldom left my home.

Mom was looking for help for me. Every treatment program she called, desperate to find a place that would accept me, told her that they only treated people with alcohol problems. No drug problems.

Finally, on December 14, 1981, she told me about a treatment program in Sebastopol, California. I listened. A year earlier, I'd made a trip to Sebastopol, fifty miles north of San Francisco, to look at a university that I was considering for my bachelor's degree. As I drove through the small town, I was taken back to the summer of 1969 when I ran away to Big Sur. I'd fallen in love with Northern California—the smell of it, the chill in the air, the magnificence of the ancient trees. I loved the time I spent alone watching the ocean and listening to the crash of waves against the rugged rocky shore. My happiest times had been when I was a little hippie, surrounded by kindness, music, and optimism. I remembered it as a happy time, before the derailing consequences of my choices.

It was because of that faint, sweet memory of Northern California that I listened and said, without thinking any further, "OK, I'll go." I was twenty-seven.

It was a choice made in a moment, with little thought. A choice like the one I made at fourteen, when I took the Seconal offered to me in the schoolyard, or all the times I returned to Anne, or when I started school to escape the life I feared, or the choice I made when I broke my promise to never use a needle. Most choices were not sought or studied. Some saved my life. Some almost destroyed it. I agreed to go to treatment in Sebastopol because any place had to be better than where I was. I didn't consider whether or not they could help me. I just wanted some relief.

last chance

I was exhausted when I boarded the plane on the morning of December 15, 1981. I didn't think much about what lay ahead—about what treatment would be like. I thought that maybe, since it was in the wine country, rehab would consist of spending time in the orchards picking grapes. I didn't consider that a happy life might be possible. If only my life could be bearable, that would be enough.

I looked around the arrival area in San Francisco where I was to be picked up. A man approached me: "Are you Teresa?"

"Yes."

"I'm Tom from Azure Acres. Do you have any luggage?"

"No, just this." My carry-on held a scant collection of pants, tops, and underwear.

"Okay, let's go—the drive is about an hour."

He looked like someone from Northern California—loose-fitting corduroy pants, a warm-looking plaid shirt, and leather moccasin-style shoes. He was young, maybe a couple of years younger than me.

We set out for the drive in a large station wagon. Tom was relaxed and seemed like a regular guy, not clinical or stiff.

He asked me about the flight. We didn't talk much. He didn't seem judgmental when he made reference to my reason for treatment. "Cocaine, right?"

"Yes," I replied.

"It's all the same," he said "Drugs, alcohol. It doesn't make a difference."

My ease was facilitated by exhaustion and apathy. We drove an hour, through Sebastopol, past apple orchards, and then turned left onto a country road that led into a deeply forested area. Eventually we arrived at a huge, two-story redwood lodge. Smoke was rising from the stone chimney into the cold, cloudy sky. I thought that I'd never want to go back to Santa Monica.

"Come on in," Tom said. We entered a large room with several overstuffed sofas and chairs arranged around a large square table. There was a roaring fire burning in a six-foot-tall stone fireplace. "This is Teresa," Tom said, introducing me to three men and a young woman sitting near the fire. "Hi Teresa," they each chimed. "Hi," I replied, not up for any social interaction right now. I followed Tom upstairs, where the bedrooms overlooked the living room. My room was large, with a double bed and a view of pine trees and the colorless, cloudy sky. I complied when Tom instructed me to lay each of my packed items on the bed so he could look for any contraband. "You can come downstairs if you want," he said, "but you might want to rest until dinner." It was about 2:00 P.M.

"I think I'll lie down for a while." He pulled the door closed.

I didn't wake up until the next morning, still dressed in the clothes I had arrived in. There was condensation on the windows, and it was chilly. I looked in the mirror and for the first time saw how haggard I had become. I combed my short, burgundy-brown hair with my fingers, changed from my rumpled clothes, and went downstairs. The living room was warm and toasty. I could smell coffee and breakfast.

At first, I couldn't tell the difference between staff and residents. Everyone was dressed in casual clothes. Tom introduced me to the four other people in treatment. Doug looked like a well-worn fifty-something, but I learned later that he was only forty. He looked about five-foot-eight, but it was hard to be sure because his shoulders were hunched in a defeated posture. His dark hair needed a cut and shampoo. Clothes hung loosely on his skinny frame, and his hands trembled so much that the coffee in his mug splashed on the floor as he walked to the table. "Welcome, glad you're here," he said, looking at me with watery eyes and a small smile. Jim looked about my age, maybe a couple of years older. My first impression was of a blue-collar guy who probably spent most evenings drinking too much beer in a small-town bar with his friends. "Hi Teresa," he said. Lori was young, under twenty, slender with long dark-blond hair. She looked as though life hadn't yet taken a toll. "Hi," she said in a bouncy way. Clarence didn't make eye contact with me and mumbled a small hello. Even seated, I could see that he was tall, at least six feet, about thirty years old. He stood out from the very white group with his creamy coffee skin and afro. Clarence sat a few seats away from the others in the group.

Eggs, bacon, hot cereal, fruit, and toast were set out on a long counter in the huge dining room. There was a large percolator with hot coffee. "Help yourself," said Carol, the cook, with a warm smile as she dried her hands on a dishtowel. Everyone sat at a large wood table after they filled their plates.

Another time, in the past, I might have felt shy and nervous around all these new people, in an unfamiliar place. But my fatigue and despair mimicked calm and collected. Despair may be the wrong word. It implies that I felt something. I felt nothing. I didn't know what to expect, but I didn't care very much. Maybe we would go out to the orchards today to pick grapes.

It didn't take long to find out that harvesting fruit wasn't part of the treatment program. Classes, group therapy, and twelve-step meetings filled the days. I learned that I had to stop alcohol too. I wouldn't be successful at stopping drugs unless I stopped everything. *Damn—if I had known that, I would have gotten drunk on the plane.* I felt cheated out of my last drink. I thought of alcohol as a privilege of adulthood: legal, available, a salve for stress and a social lubricant. Everyone drank. It wasn't a problem compared to the drugs. I didn't hock the diamond ring my mother gave me when I graduated from nursing school in order to buy alcohol. The one hundred dollars I got for it bought me a gram of cocaine. I never sat in my car in a dark parking lot for an hour waiting for someone to bring me alcohol, but I'd wait forever for a drug connection to show up with enough cocaine to last me an hour.

"Alcohol and drugs are the same. You have a disease, and only complete abstinence will work," the counselor said.

A disease? Sounds like a convenient explanation to me. Not like any disease I know. Who are these people, telling me about a disease? They aren't medical professionals. Show me this disease in a medical text. I didn't buy it but figured if that's what people have to believe, so be it. Anyone reading my story can see that alcohol was a problem, but at that time, I couldn't see it.

There were seven of us in our group session and the counselor, Tom, handed out pieces of paper and pens. He instructed each of us to write down a deep, dark secret that we felt we couldn't tell anyone. Something we had been keeping inside. "Don't sign it," he said. "They are anonymous. You do not have to share them, but you may if you choose to."

My skin prickled. I knew immediately what I needed to write down. I had never told anyone, had kept it to myself since I was a little girl. If people knew what I had done, they would know that I was a horrible person.

As I sat on the floor, my piece of paper on the large table and my pen poised to write, I remembered the day:

I was young, eight or nine, and was babysitting Mikey for a couple of hours. I had been proud when my parents began to let me watch over her. It meant that they could count on me. Mikey was quiet, rocking. I was reading.

I led Mikey into the small bathroom, the one that only had a toilet and sink. I had cut a five-foot-long piece of thin, silver-colored ribbon—the kind we used to wrap presents, the thin kind that curled up tight when you slid the scissors blade across it. I tied one end loosely around Mikey's wrist and the other end around the exposed, U-shaped pipe under the sink. Mikey sat, rocking quietly as I watched her. After a minute or two, she tried to stand up to leave the bathroom, but the ribbon held her back. She didn't seem perturbed, just sat back down and began to rock. I was ashamed at that moment about what I had done. I cut the ribbon so she could move freely. And I tucked my secret away where I would hide it until that day in the group session when I wrote: "I tied up my handicapped sister when we were children."

I decided that I would read my secret to the group. I wanted to get it out—no matter what they thought of me. I watched their faces when I spoke, looking for signs of their disgust. But no one seemed to be horrified. I don't remember precisely what anyone said, but I know they didn't tell me that I was bad. In fact, they seemed rather unfazed. Perhaps everyone was thinking about their own secrets and struggling with whether or not they would tell on themselves.

I felt relieved to share, finally, the thing that made me most ashamed of myself.

It was on a cold Tuesday night that Diane, the program director's girlfriend, drove the two of us into Santa Rosa, a few miles from Sebastopol. We pulled up to a tiny church with a white steeple that sat alone on an empty road. Light shone from the open door. There were a couple of pickup trucks and a few cars parked in the parking lot. Three men stood outside the door smoking cigarettes. Diane and I crunched across the gravel parking lot, entered the church, and sat in a pew toward the back. There were no other women in the room. The meeting was called to order. Two men sat up front, facing everyone else. One was called the secretary. The other was the speaker. Before the speaker began, someone in the audience read a paragraph from a little pamphlet that described what it is like to be an addict.

That's me, I thought. The rest of the reading and most of

what the speaker shared was a blur to me. When the meeting ended, two of the men came over to welcome me and encouraged me to come back.

These people got it. They had felt and acted the way I did. They didn't look as fancy as the people from the meetings at Azure Acres, but they welcomed me. Some were ex-convicts, but none of them seemed to be loaded. I wondered if they were really able to stop using everything—really quit—or if they tried to reduce and control use. *Was this a safe place?* I wondered. I didn't know any drug addicts who stopped, and I thought that drugs might be available at the meetings. I knew I couldn't be around drugs without using.

I decided that I would try complete abstinence for one year. If I hated it, I would drink. I completed thirty days of treatment at Azure Acres and moved into a small shack in a country setting just outside Sebastopol. I knew I had to leave everyone in Southern California behind if I was going to survive. I had barely enough money for rent. As long as I had enough for essentials —coffee, cigarettes, dog food for Maxi, and toilet paper—I was okay. Sometimes I had to search for change that had fallen under my car seat or sofa cushions to gather enough for gas. Or choose between gas and cigarettes. I needed gas to get to meetings every day. Uncomfortable and shy, I made myself go to meetings and spend an hour with strangers who would teach me how to stay off drugs.

I thought about drugs, dreamed about fixing. Craved when I heard certain songs. But I didn't use. I used slogans, meetings, and phone calls to other recovering people to get through it.

I visited my parents in Santa Monica, and they came to Santa Rosa to see me. They were forgiving and supportive. I saw Anne a couple of times when in Southern California. She was drinking a lot. I loved her and wanted to help her. I took her to a couple of meetings and encouraged her to go into treatment. Wouldn't it be great if we could be sober together? But I knew that I couldn't linger in Southern California. It was too dangerous for me. I wouldn't be able to resist the urge to drink or use. So

I returned to Northern California, time passed, and Anne and I were no longer in touch. We finally went our separate ways.

When I had two years of abstinence under my belt, I began work at a new hospital-based drug and alcohol treatment center. It was perfect. I learned about medical detoxification. I understood the anxiety and fear that the patients felt and could comfort them, could help them find hope. Over the course of two years, I was promoted to program director. Cocaine use continued to be rampant in all levels of society, and research began to focus on addiction. Over the coming years, a neurological basis for drug and alcohol addiction would be confirmed.

I loved Sonoma County—work, school, Wednesday night dinners with my best friend Renee, and poker at my house after the Friday night meeting. One important factor made it possible for me to stay. Each time I drove from Santa Rosa to Sonoma I passed a large state developmental center. It was a facility like Fairview where Mikey lived. I knew that I would one day be the only person who could be Mikey's protector and advocate and that I would always need to live near her. When my parents passed away, I would have her transferred to be close to me.

But, in spite of everything that was good about Sonoma County, I decided in 1986, after nearly five years of recovery, to move back to Santa Monica. I had come to realize that the city wasn't going to kill me; the disease of addiction was the enemy. I had finally crossed the bridge between self-destruction and survival. I accepted that I would never again feel the seductive, drug-induced euphoria that had both enticed and trapped me. I couldn't use substances for comfort or courage. The world where I once found fun, escape, and relief was off-limits to me.

Instead, I had tools and support. I had learned how to live without drugs and alcohol, how to make friends. There would be meetings in Southern California. I wanted to be closer to my parents. Now that Mom didn't have to worry about me, we had become good friends. She was seventy years old now. I could help with Mikey. And I wanted more career opportunities.

reunion

On October 24, 1992, I received a phone call from Anne. We were thirty-eight. I had been drug-free for nearly eleven years. During that time, I finished my bachelor's degree in organizational behavior, traveled throughout New England teaching drug education in prep schools, and married John, a recovering alcoholic, whom I divorced three years later. As my cousin John once said to me, "Lucky in cards, unlucky in love." Now, I was the program director at a drug treatment program in Marina del Rey, and engaged to Craig, a counselor. I was content.

Anne explained that she and her husband, Michael, were in Santa Monica from Oakland, where they were living, to visit her dad. "Did you know that our twenty-year high school reunion is tonight?" she asked. "It's at the carousel on the pier. Do you want to go?"

Because I didn't graduate with my class, I wasn't aware of such events, and there was no one else to keep me informed.

"No, I didn't know and, yes, I definitely want to go!" I responded. I felt my skin prickle with excitement. Here we were, a pair of rebels who had survived our dance on the dark side and made lives for ourselves. Tonight we would revisit our old stomping grounds. It felt like a victory celebration. There was no question that we wouldn't be taking her husband or my fiancé. It was just the two of us again. We arranged to meet at her father's house at around 6:00 P.M.

I told my fiancé, Craig, about my plans and about Anne. "That's nice. Have a good time," he said, uninterested.

What to wear? I spent my days in suits and heels. Nurses and counselors that I worked with knew that I was recovering; I worked in treatment, after all. But administrators—straight people—had no need to know. For this occasion, I wanted my normalness to shine, but with a touch of the old hippie that would always be part of me.

I picked a long brown lace dress, fashionable but certainly not conservative. Nice but not too dressy. A brown felt fedora made the outfit just a little bit quirky.

Anne and I hugged when she opened the door at her father's house, and I came into the living room. Her father and stepmother greeted me warmly. Anne looked pretty. She had never been able to grow her hair long, but now it was well below her shoulders. Contacts had replaced glasses. She was also wearing a long dress that complimented her petite frame, and a vest that made her outfit her own.

The house, the room, and the people all felt so familiar but also different. Of course, we were older now, more mature. Anne and I had each followed a path away from destruction, but our lives had not been intertwined for a decade. I felt the affection between us and the bond of our shared experiences would never be broken, but there was separateness, too. A healthy separateness, I suppose.

"What do you think?" I asked everyone. "Should I wear my hat or not?" The vote was unanimous—wear it.

We had time before arriving at the pier to catch up on our lives. She was married, lived in Oakland, and worked as an administrative assistant. She had stopped drinking years ago. I can't explain exactly why I was surprised by how successful her transformation was. She was confident and grounded. I was happy for her. A little voice said, *Maybe you didn't have to break ties so completely. Maybe you could have been friends all these years.* But I knew that I would never have survived if I hadn't made the break from everyone, at least in the beginning of my recovery.

We reminisced a little about the old days—the days before everything fell apart. "Remember the time we lost our car in the parking lot at the Rod Stewart concert?" she asked.

"Oh yeah," I laughed.

Not surprisingly, we recounted some of our LSD moments. "Remember the snails?" I asked.

"Oh my God, yes! How about when we lit the plastic dry cleaning bag and watched the colors?"

"No, I don't remember," I said, sad that I was missing a memory and hoping that I wouldn't break the thread of our renewed connection.

The carousel was the perfect place for our reunion. We had so much history there.

There were a few people that I remembered from elementary school. Some were drunk, some balding. Many seemed happy to see each other. I reminisced with Jill, from junior high, about slumber parties. "What are you doing these days?" I asked her.

"Oh, my husband and I had five kids, and we own an accounting firm. How about you?"

"I lived in Northern California for a while. I've been doing the career thing." There was no need to tell it all. Sometimes I wonder if I am more shocked by my life, the dark part, than other people would be.

I looked for Lydia and Sharlon, friends that I had discarded years ago when Anne became my only and best friend, but they weren't there. I miss them both and am ashamed of how thoughtless I was. I don't know how much it mattered to them, but I think it did.

The night after the reunion, Anne, Michael, Craig, and I went out to dinner. Michael was excited about a new business venture he was beginning. Craig was distracted, bordering on rudeness. It was obvious that he was impatient for the evening to end.

The next morning, on the phone, Anne told me that she and Michael had both been hurt by Craig's cold manner. I knew that his apparent disdain compromised my chances for a renewed friendship with Anne. I defended him. I regret it now. Anne and I said good-bye. I don't remember if we said anything about staying in touch. It was the last time I spoke to her. I was busy with my life. I didn't try to locate her and I didn't notice the passage of time.

She died three years later but I didn't learn about it until I saw her father one day at a garage sale many years later.

I recognized him right away, looking at tools that were arranged on a blanket spread out on the front lawn. He looked unchanged—tall and lanky, square-jawed, wearing glasses. I approached, and he smiled. His manner was relaxed.

"Hi, Mr. Nelson." I asked him how Anne was doing. "I haven't spoken with her for a long time."

"Anne and her husband died in a car accident ten years ago."

My face remained placid, but my heart skipped. *How is this possible?* I should have known the moment she died. I should have felt it in my gut or dreamed about her. How could I not know that she was gone?

"I'm so sorry," I said.

He told me that Anne and her husband, Michael, were on their way from California to Texas in 1995. Anne was driving and, as she was changing lanes, clipped a semi-tractor-trailer. Their deaths were instant. I thought, *Of course, it would be a car accident that killed her.* "Is she buried at Woodlawn Cemetery?" I asked. I wanted to visit her grave.

"No," he said. "Her ashes are in my attic." He had had time to grieve and to accept her death. But for me, it was as if she had died only yesterday.

Then, I pulled myself back to the present moment.

I asked about his other daughters and wished him well. I didn't linger any longer.

If I hadn't come with a friend, I might have parked a short distance away, out of sight, and sat alone for a while. Instead, I moved on with my day, casually explaining to my friend that Anne had been my best friend when we were young.

red satchel

Just as my journey had not been a smooth one, neither had Mikey's. By the time she was forty, after more than twenty years at Fairview, budget cuts had severely compromised the quality of her care. The unit for blind girls no longer existed. Instead, Mikey was on a unit with severely handicapped men and women. Not all were blind, and many were in wheelchairs. Mikey spent more time rocking in a chair—it was impossible to navigate safely in a corridor filled with wheelchairs. She continued to have outbursts.

I was more inclined to make waves. I was her co-conservator, and because I was a nurse, it was harder for the staff and doctors to ignore me when I demanded that attention be paid to her weight loss or when her behavior suggested something in particular was troubling her. The staff response was disappointing. Their hands were tied by budget limitations and by unit conditions that couldn't be changed. Sometimes they were clearly annoyed by my repeated questions and demands. I challenged their approach to her unstable weight. "What is the point of giving her double portions of food when she doesn't eat? You need to try something else!" When Mikey seemed confused, I said,

"Something is wrong. I know my sister. This isn't normal for her." They ignored me until Mikey became more unsteady and ended up in the hospital due to a drug reaction.

I know other clients had visitors, people who cared deeply for them, but we seldom saw other family members when we visited Mikey. Parents had passed away or become too fragile to manage the trip. Siblings had moved on with their lives. I remember one day, watching a line of residents being herded back into their unit by a couple of staff members. It reminded me of the animal shelter. I thought of dogs that no one came to visit, animals that were invisible to the outside world, forgotten, languishing in their kennels.

In spite of my busy career as a hospital administrator, I made time to take my mother to see Mikey at least once a month. Dad's life had become more removed from ours. His drinking had cost him his job and was taking a toll on his health.

One visit to see Mikey stands out:

It was 1995. Mikey was forty-two, and Mom was eighty. Mom kept a large red satchel in the trunk of her car. It had small wheels on the bottom, stood about two feet tall, and was filled with toys, dishes, scented body lotion, a cotton hospital gown, transistor radio, and other miscellaneous items for a visit. Around 11:00 A.M., after transferring the satchel to my car, we headed south for the hour-long drive to Fairview.

Before picking up Mikey, we stopped at Kentucky Fried Chicken, and then went to an inexpensive motel near Fairview to rent a room for the day. Typically, motels won't rent a room for a partial day, but the managers knew Mom from previous visits. Our room was on the ground floor. It was plain, with cheap furnishings. But the appearance was insignificant. As long as it had a bed and a bathtub, it met our purposes. I carried the red satchel and the box of chicken into the room while Mom checked to make sure the stopper in the bathtub worked. If we couldn't fill the tub, we would ask for a different room.

When we arrived at her unit at Fairview, Mikey made a

beeline for Mom's voice as soon as she heard it. Her face lit up, and she rocked as she walked toward us with a wide-based gait and her arm outstretched to reach Mom. I saw how frail they both were and knew that soon I would be the only person left who cared about Mikey.

"There's my Mikey," Mom said, giving her a beacon to guide her. Mikey held as still as she could while Mom bent to kiss her cheek. Then it was time to go!

"Step down." I held Mikey's arm lightly as we went down the curb toward the car.

"Watch your head, Mikey," as I helped her into the passenger seat. She was more docile now. We no longer needed latches on the outside of the car doors.

When we arrived back at the room, Mikey sat on the edge of one of the beds, rocking and smiling. I went into the bathroom and turned the water on to fill the tub. As soon as she heard the rush of water, she stood up, giggling, and turned toward the sound.

"Wait a minute, Mikey," Mom said.

Mikey sat back down—making happy sounds.

Mom helped her undress and inspected her body. When the tub was full, she guided her into the bathroom.

As soon as she sat down in the tub, Mikey slid down till the water was just under her chin. I stayed in the bathroom with her while Mom emptied the red satchel in the other room. Mikey reached up to turn the water on. Her face stilled, and she cocked her head at the sound of the rushing water and held her hand under the faucet. I made sure it wasn't too hot. After fifteen minutes, I helped Mikey out of the tub. She cooperated while I dried her and put on the old, faded cotton hospital gown.

Mom had pulled white meat chicken breast from the bones and placed the pieces on the plastic plate we brought with us. She added a small cob of corn and cantaloupe from home.

Mikey sat at the desk, her legs pulled up, knees under her chin, and felt for the food that was set out on the plate in front of her. After she had finished eating, Mom held her hand and

guided her to the bed. Now they would have their Mom and Mikey time. First, Mom rubbed a dab of perfumed lotion on Mikey's wrist. Mikey looked enchanted as she held her wrist to her nose and inhaled the scent. She leaned back onto Mom's lap. Thinking back to that moment, I can feel the magic of their connection. Mom was soft and affectionate, and Mikey was safe and relaxed. It was only when they were with each other that I ever saw either of them that way. Occasionally, Mikey brought her wrist back to her nose to smell the perfume.

I reclined on the other bed reading and, when quiet time was over, thirty minutes later, I joined in. I handed Mikey a talking doll, and she giggled each time she pulled the string and the doll said, "Hello, my name is Kathy, what's your name?"

"Let's try the Jacuzzi," Mom said. I walked outside and when I came back to the room told Mom, "It's empty and nice and warm." Mom dressed Mikey in a two-piece swimsuit.

I stepped into the swirling water first and guided Mikey as

Mom transferred her to me. Mikey stood right in the middle, up to her waist, and held still for a moment. I guided her to the seat. After a few moments, she stood up again then plunged under the water. We waited and waited. Mom and I exchanged looks. Was something wrong? Just before I went under for her, Mikey burst through the water laughing—exhilarated. She did it over and over.

Finally, we packed up and took Mikey back to her unit. It had been a good visit.

mikey

On Saturday night, October 11, 1997, I was at my home in Palm Springs, my weekend refuge from a typically demanding week climbing the career ladder. I was forty-three. Craig and I had divorced in 1994, less than three years after marrying; I bought a home in Santa Monica and, in 1996, completed my MBA.

I had made the two-hour drive to Palm Springs from Santa Monica on Friday evening with my friend and colleague Beverly. Bev and I had worked together for eight years as administrators for addiction and mental health programs. We had become closer friends over the past two when we divorced within a year of each other. We began to spend some of our newly acquired free time together and discovered that we had more in common than work: responsibility for siblings at a young age and a measure of wildness in our twenties. We even went to the same nursing school a year apart in order to save our on-the-brink-of-disaster lives.

Bev and I were prosperous and independent. We were particularly amused to discover the many qualities our ex-husbands shared, although hers didn't have a penchant for lap dances and prostitutes, as mine did.

Bev was pragmatic. A year earlier, she had been efficiently supportive, not overly solicitous, when she helped my mother and me take my father to the hospital when he had a stroke during a luncheon.

It was about 9:00 P.M. and after a leisurely day shopping and lunching, we were in for the night. Bev was in the guest bedroom, and I was in my room reading *What to Expect When You're Expecting*— I had been happily shocked three weeks previously when I discovered that I was pregnant. Maybe it was hormones, or an instrinsic maternal phenomenon that had washed away my fear of having a child like Mikey. I was strong, capable, and in a stable relationship with Ron, a psychologist and colleague. That said, given my history of short-term commitment, I knew I might become a single parent. I was all right with that.

The phone rang. It was Mom.

"Teresa, Mikey's dead." Her voice was calm and measured.

"What?" Shocked, I stood up. Bev called out from her room, "Are you OK?"

I was standing near the foot of the bed waiting for Mom to tell me more when Bev came to my door and waited quietly.

"They found her not breathing. Her body is at Hoag Hospital," Mom said.

"What the hell happened?"

"I don't have any details, only that they took her to Hoag Memorial Hospital."

"I'm leaving now. I'll pick you up," I told her.

There was no need to discuss whether or not we would go to the hospital. We understood without words that we had to be with Mikey.

I was equidistant from Mom's place in Santa Monica and the hospital in Newport Beach. When I called Ron to tell him what had happened, he offered to pick up my mother and meet me at the hospital. It would save us hours. I let Mom know, and then called the hospital to get directions.

Before leaving to meet Mom, I stood quietly, alone in my

room, for a few moments. I thought, *maybe she had a choice in her death, just as I had so many years ago. Maybe her soul would choose my child for its next life. I would love her and keep her safe. She could have a life completely unlike the one she had known.* It was a sweet, hopeful thought.

A split second later I thought, *I'm free. I can live anywhere now.* My future had become mine in a new way, untethered from the responsibility to always live near a developmental center, and to someday be Mikey's only family and advocate. It was a responsibility I had accepted without resentment. I didn't think further about it at that moment.

I handed Bev the written directions, put my dachshund, Roxy, in the back seat, and got behind the wheel of my Lexus. It was dark as we drove through the desert. There were stretches when it seemed that we were the only car on the road.

After driving for what seemed too long, I asked Bev, "Did we pass a connection? Are we lost?" It seemed like it was taking forever, and Mom needed me to be there. The anxiety of the drive distracted me from thinking about Mikey. I looked into the darkness, both hands on the steering wheel, depending on Bev to get us there.

I wasn't going to fall apart now, and I didn't need a shoulder to cry on. I needed someone who would make it easier to get where I needed to be.

Our drive to the hospital where Mikey and my mother waited was eerily similar to trips our family had taken when I was a child, when we started out at night on lonely roads.

I thought about the last time I saw Mikey. It was only two weeks earlier. I had gone to see her by myself. It may have been the only time I went alone. We sat at the picnic table outside her unit for about an hour. After she had enjoyed some of her favorite foods, we sat together and she listened to the transistor radio I had brought. I remembered so vividly bending down on one knee to tie her well-washed white sneakers, as I had done hundreds of times before, and then taking her hand and guiding her back to her unit. She was docile and cooperative as I transferred her to the staff member who opened the door. She held still as I kissed her on the cheek and said, "Good-bye, Mikey."

Finally, city lights emerged. We must be close. It seemed like it had taken us two hours.

Someone directed us to the emergency room, where Mom and Ron were sitting on plastic chairs outside the double doors. Ron was wearing a wool cap. When he removed it, I saw that he had shaved his balding head. I felt a flash of anger at myself, regretting that I hadn't picked up Mom myself. She barely knew Ron, and it should have been me that made the long drive with her.

We rang a bell, and a staff member opened the doors and showed us to the room where Mikey was. She was lying on a sheet-covered metal gurney in the middle of the brightly lit room. Her face was ashen, her hair disheveled, and her eyes closed. There was a breathing tube sticking out of her mouth. The nurse explained that, in a coroner's case, the hospital staff wasn't permitted to remove tubing or other apparatus. She left the room and closed the door behind her. Mikey looked small and fragile lying under the thin sheet, her bare feet exposed.

A sob escaped my lips, and my chest heaved. For a moment, it was only Mikey and me in the room. I was unaware of anyone else. Ron moved behind me and put his arms around my waist. Then I saw that Mom was slowly circling Mikey's body with an intense look on her face, as though an answer would reveal itself if only she concentrated hard enough. The answer to how Mikey had died. Bev stood back, inconspicuous, against a wall. "She is better off now," I murmured, mostly to myself.

Mom glared at me for just a split second. Perhaps only a mother is entitled to say those words. Who else has the right to make such a judgment? But I believed she was better off. I was relieved for her. Perhaps my thoughts from earlier that evening, hoping that her spirit was still with me, made it easier to say.

Mom and I didn't comfort each other with touch or words. Maybe if we had been alone in the room with Mikey we would have, but that wasn't our way.

After thirty minutes, the nurse re-entered and told us that Mikey's body was being released to the coroner and would be transported to the morgue. The doctor who had pronounced Mikey dead explained that when paramedics arrived at Fairview, Mikey still had some cardiac electrical activity. They tried to resuscitate her but were unable to. We didn't have any information about why she had stopped breathing.

Mom and I drove home together. Ron took Bev. It was good to be alone with Mom. We were going to put one foot in front of the other, together, and handle this. Get answers, demand accountability, explain it to my father, and bury Mikey.

little darling

The day after Mikey died I contacted the coroner's office. There would be an autopsy. I asked them to check if she had been pregnant. If a technician at Fairview had been molesting her, fear of pregnancy might be motivation for murder. I asked to check for signs of suffocation but realized later that it was impossible to see the little broken blood vessels in her eyes that would support that finding.

The coroner released her body on October 16, 1997, five days following her death.

The death certificate said "pending investigation" in the box for the cause of death. The coroner's office told us we would be informed of the final autopsy findings when they had finished analyzing the information they had gathered.

We had a viewing at the mortuary—a couple of hours to sit quietly one last time with Mikey. Mom and I decided not to embalm her. We could protect her from one final assault. Sconces lit the small room with soft light. There were plush couches and chairs. Mom had picked out a pretty dress for Mikey, dark blue with tiny flowers. I saw that she had a prominent bruise on the bridge of her nose that I hadn't noticed at the hospital. Her lips were chapped. Dad had recovered pretty well from his stroke. No paralysis and his speech was fine but he wasn't very oriented to the passage of time. He understood what was happening and sobbed. Mom was quiet, standing near the casket looking at Mikey. She took some pictures. I had tied a ribbon around a tin can lid and placed it under Mikey's cold, folded hands.

A Lutheran minister said some words at the graveside. Mom had told him stories about Mikey. He did a pretty good job. My aunt and cousins stood around the grave, too. Ron stood next to me. I thought about the child I carried and hoped again that Mikey would stay with me.

Three weeks later, when I had my first ultrasound, there was no heartbeat. There would be no child. The D&C that followed was painful. I cramped and spotted for days.

I grieved privately. It was final now—Mikey was gone. The thought crossed my mind that the stress of Mikey's death might have caused my miscarriage, and I was angry with her—but only for a moment. Since her death, my feelings had been raw and conflicted: grief, relief, anger, sorrow. I didn't share them with anyone. I escaped my pain by attending to the tasks of death—funeral arrangements and death certificates.

As Mikey's co-conservator, I had access to her medical records, and I reviewed the events of that night thoroughly. The incompetence, delays, and negligence that followed read like a Three Stooges movie. No CPR for ten minutes. No one knew how to operate the oxygen tank. No one called for help according to hospital protocol. I reported the incident to the Department of Health.

The coroner's examination of Mikey's brain and spinal cord wasn't completed until March 1, 1998—nearly five months after her death. The amended autopsy report was dated May 7, 1998, over two months later. The cause of death was: "Epileptic Seizure Disorder, Clinical," which meant they didn't identify a cause, but instead listed a medical diagnosis she was known to have. There was no notation in her medical records that she had a seizure on the day she died.

The autopsy described Mikey as a "profoundly retarded" woman. It was the diagnosis she carried throughout her time at Fairview. Her brain weighed 1020 grams—less than the average adult female brain (1198 grams).

Of particular note is the finding: Spinal Cord: Central cord necrosis, acute.

Fairview officials refused for nine months to address our questions about Mikey's death. Trying to force a response, Mom and I filed a claim, a prerequisite to a lawsuit. Then we learned that we could not pursue it because six months had passed while we were waiting for the autopsy results. It seemed odd that the autopsy was delayed until shortly after the deadline for taking action against the state had passed. I wondered if there had been collusion. Mom and I met with an attorney about a wrongful death suit—not because we were interested in collecting money but because we couldn't accept her death being swept under the carpet. The attorney informed us that no one would be interested in taking the case. Wrongful death awards are based on the deceased person's value as an earner. By that math, Mikey wasn't worth anything.

The State Department of Developmental Services conducted an independent investigation:

"This preliminary investigation and review of the evidence obtained from the interviews and documentation support a finding of neglect," the investigator reported. She also reported discrepancies between what different staff members noted in Mikey's medical chart. The investigator's findings were forwarded to the Orange County district attorney's office homicide unit to determine if charges should be filed. No charges were ever filed. Two of the employees were terminated.

We never knew why Mikey was found unresponsive.

Nearly a year after she died, Mom and I had one more opportunity to represent Mikey—to tell her story. I contacted the *Orange County Register* to see if they would be interested. The journalist interviewed Mom and Fairview administrators as well as me. He reviewed investigative reports. The story appeared on the front page.

Excerpts:

*RELATIVES QUESTION DEATH AT
FAIRVIEW PROBE:*

*The state says the staff failed to provide prompt
lifesaving aid.*
   *Crucial minutes ticked away last Oct. 11
as Michele Sullivan lay in her bed at Fairview
Developmental Center, unresponsive and turning blue
while three trained staff members did little to help after
they found her.*
   *Fairview Executive Director described the
situation as unprecedented during his time at the
institution and said he is mystified by the staff's actions.*
   *Fairview's Clinical director declined to discuss
Sullivan's case in detail, citing the state's investigation.*
   *The Sullivans say that after 25 years spent heavily
involved in Michele's care and trying to protect her,
they cannot accept the way she died. "Ever since her
death, particularly when we were told we couldn't ask
questions, I have been thinking about that line from
'Death of a Salesman'—'Attention must be paid,'"
Marcile Sullivan said.*
   *Like the life of Willy Loman, the downward-
spiraling character in Arthur Miller's play, the lives
of her daughter and other developmentally disabled
people might seem insignificant to some, she said. "But
these aren't throwaway people," she said. "People have
to care whether they get proper attention. Attention
must be paid."*

Over fifteen years after Mikey's death, in order to verify
information for this book, I requested another copy of her autopsy
report. There was an addendum dated October 1998 that I had

never seen. The addendum was added one month after Mikey's story appeared in the *Orange County Register*. The same pathologist who had completed the initial brain examination stated that, upon further examination, the spinal cord was normal. Did the medical examiner close the case by altering her findings? I will never know.

When making burial arrangements, we chose a simple remembrance card and included lyrics from George Harrison's song "Here Comes the Sun." I like to think that after the long, dark winter that was her life, she is dancing in the sun.

MICHELE COLLEEN SULLIVAN
BORN: FEBRUARY 2, 1953
PASSED: OCTOBER 11, 1997

afterword

It goes without saying that Mom's life changed after Mikey was gone. It may not have been obvious to others—Mom didn't talk about her feelings or draw attention to herself. She loved gardening, and her flowers continued to thrive. As the matriarch of our family, her support of and interest in me, my cousins, and her sister, Phyllis, remained unchanged. But I had always known how profoundly Mom would be affected if she outlived Mikey. There was a void where there had once been a purpose. She no longer had a reason to look for ways to make Mikey's life better, to comfort and advocate for her. She no longer needed to ask Phyllis or me to drive her to see Mikey and take her to a hotel, visits that could encompass an entire day. For forty-four years, Mikey and her needs had been the center of Mom's heart and thoughts.

Mom and I were close. Every morning, I took my young dachshund, Roxy, to Mom's house, and she took care of her while I worked long hours. They walked several times a day and visited with neighbors they met along the way. Looking back, I think that Roxy's affection and dependence sometimes helped Mom get up and dressed. A year later, I got another dachshund, Ginger, and Mom drove two blocks to my house every day to babysit. We all needed her.

Mom passed away in June 2003, four and a half years after Mikey died. She was eighty-seven.

Dad had been in an assisted living residence since his stroke in 1996. Shortly before Mikey's death, following a fall and hip fracture, he was transferred to a nursing home. Mom and I used to pick him up to take him out to dinner. Although they were separated for over thirty years, they never divorced.

One night, Dad walked away from his facility and couldn't be found. It seems profoundly ironic that he wandered into an AA meeting. A kind man read the band on his wrist and brought him back to the nursing home. I had to place him in a locked facility. It was a pleasant place, with lots of activities. I visited him every weekend.

One day when I was taking Dad for a doctor's appointment at the Veterans Administration, I unloaded the wheelchair from the trunk of my car and helped him out of the passenger seat. It was warm, and as I looked up at a clear blue sky, a thought crossed my mind. Perhaps many women who don't have children have a similar moment of realization:

Here I am—it's too late to have a child, a family of my own. I didn't notice the passage of time. But, in a way, I have always been a parent, and it is enough.

Dad's memory continued to get worse. Sometimes he'd ask, "How's your mother?" Initially, I'd remind him that she had died, but after a while I told him that she was doing well. In his mind, he was often living in the 1940s, maybe the happiest time in his life. I stopped trying to talk him out of it. It seems to be true that, as a person grows older, their true nature emerges. My father's temperament was sweet. He was a gentle man. He passed away in June 2004 at the age of eighty-four, six days short of a year after Mom died.

Mikey, Mom, and Dad are all buried at Woodlawn Cemetery in Santa Monica. I sometimes visit, though not as often now. I miss them and feel a deep compassion for all of us.

Ron and I split up a few months after Mikey's death. I tried another relationship, but it ended after a couple of years. At that time I left hospital administration and returned to clinical work as Director of an addiction treatment program in Malibu.

I had proven something to myself through my degrees, salaries, and titles. I achieved success by many measures, and it was challenging and mentally stimulating. But it was helping others that fed my soul. Back when I was twenty-five and working as a nurse at UCLA, I discovered a Ralph Waldo Emerson quote in a magazine. I cut it out and have kept it all these years:

To know even one life has breathed easier because you have lived. This is to have succeeded.

If there has been a purpose to my surviving the motorcycle accident, it was to learn this lesson.

I am still drug- and alcohol-free. Sometimes, in a certain light, I notice the faded scar on my left arm—an indentation above the vein I used most often to inject drugs. A reminder: *I survived!*

I'm not ashamed of the dark part of my past, but I generally only speak about the drama, drunkenness, drugs, and despair with good friends or with people who might gain hope or be helped by my experience. Most of the people who traveled that road with me are dead and gone. Most died before they were forty. There are only a couple of us who managed to climb out of the rabbit hole. Mark, my boyfriend from high school, is one of the survivors. We talk occasionally.

I have residual effects from the motorcycle accident: a slight limp, I can't quite close my left eye, and I drop things. I developed a mild form of epilepsy. When a seizure begins, my initial response is, "Damn!" I feel angry that I have epilepsy and afraid that it will get worse. When it's over, about a minute later, I remind myself to view the seizure in light of what could have been.

Mikey and my family shaped me profoundly. As a child, I put aside my feelings and needs in order to be part of a team with a common purpose—to help Mikey. We all did. This dynamic planted the seeds of selflessness, compassion, and cooperation, but also had residual consequences that I ultimately had to address. It took years for me to realize that selflessness has its own dangers. In excess, it may be a form of self-betrayal. Expecting nothing isn't strength, nor does it bring affection.

I witnessed my parents' unwavering perseverance in the face of adversity, a quality that helped me recover from my traumatic accident and my addiction.

I would do anything to erase the suffering Mikey endured, but I would not alter how she influenced who I became.

When I'm feeling upset with the challenges of a day—traffic, a headache, not enough money to do what I want, friends not acting the way I want, or even more serious problems like health concerns—I feel tense and preoccupied with my dissatisfactions. Then, an image of Mikey flashes across my mind—just her face, not necessarily a specific memory. In that moment, my problems seem insignificant, and I feel something close to shame for being so absorbed by them. Everything is put in perspective. As the moment passes, I resume my day feeling humbled and fortunate.

Sometimes, when I'm alone, I cry about the tragedy of her life. I'm haunted by painful memories. But I can also call upon sweet times, happy twirling, strawberries, and nighttime car rides for donuts.

post script

Eighteen years after Mikey died, I saw on the news that the state of California planned to close Fairview Developmental Center and transition its residents into smaller privately run community facilities. The only people still residing there were the most impaired. Mikey would have been one of them.

The state insisted that the move was necessary because they were required to transition residents to the least restrictive setting, less institutional environments. But I knew that Fairview was a line item in the state budget. The residents weren't real to legislators. They were invisible, and the few family members had no lobbyists to represent them.

I hadn't had anything to do with Fairview since Mikey's death, but I wanted to support the families. So I went to a Fairview Families and Friends meeting. This group was just as protective—and afraid—about the treatment of their vulnerable loved ones as my parents and I had been about Mikey, and were losing the security of knowing that their loved ones had a place for the rest of their lives. It must seem impossible that I would push for Fairview to remain open after the way Mikey died, but

I know through my professional experience what happens to people like her when a private facility is unequipped to handle violent behavior. Patients end up in locked psychiatric units and are treated by staff untrained in the management of neurodevelopmental disorders. Reminiscent of Camarillo, restraints and injections are relied upon.

I sensed the resignation of many of the Fairview families. They had been fighting for their loved ones for years, maybe decades. I was one of them. They welcomed me with open arms.

The state representative followed his script at the meeting and gave a spiel about how the Fairview residents would benefit from the transition. Family members asked questions with a portable microphone, expressing their doubts and fears. I weighed whether to keep quiet or share my experience before deciding to speak up. Would it be helpful or harmful? Taking the microphone, I outlined the very real dangers the patients at Fairview faced with the impending move. I was unwilling to condone the state's whitewash of the reasons behind the closing. "Someone needs to be held accountable!" I said. The families applauded. They appreciated hearing naked truth.

"We acknowledge that there will be gaps in services," the state representative said. In other words, the most vulnerable would fall through the cracks as a result of the transition, likely not receive the services they need, and suffer the consequences.

I feel so deeply sorry for these families, and grateful that Mikey died before we were put in this untenable situation.

I met siblings that day, advocating for their brothers and sisters. It was my first contact with others whose childhood had been like mine. I so wish I had known them while I was growing up.

Solitude has never been difficult for me. I find it soothing to be away from the cacophony of the world. But I need connection, too, and it has been elusive. So often I had wondered, *Where do I fit in?* Living with Mikey prepared me for simultaneously occupying disparate universes—the outside world and my family, the conventional world and the counterculture, the professional world and my addiction. I don't feel the discomfort of being an outsider anymore. I move freely in different groups and situations, knowing who I am within each.

But a sense of true belonging, of fitting in with such ease that I never have to wonder what to do or how to be, is still rare. I felt it with my family before Mikey left. I felt it with Anne. And I felt it that day in the Fairview Families and Friends meeting. We have had tragedy in common, but we have celebrated victories that others may take for granted: toilet training when it had seemed impossible, a simple spoken word, a day without violence. We have been grateful for each expression of kindness from an outsider and enraged by acts of cruelty. We have felt invisible, afraid of the future, and powerless against an indifferent bureaucracy that saw numbers where we saw vulnerable sons and daughters, brothers and sisters whom we loved from the depths of our being. Among these people, I will always belong. They are family.

acknowledgments

I would like to thank Margot Dougherty, my incredible editor, for her expertise and sensitivity. Amy Friedman, my first memoir teacher, for direction, encouragement and for introducing me to my editor and to She Writes Press. Michela F. Gunn, MD, for helping me through the tears and sometimes the terror of memories. Crystal Patriarche, CEO, and Korina Garcia, PR Lead, at BookSparks for all the things that publicists do. Bob Sullivan, my cousin, for asking to read and trudging through the unformatted, soft version of *Mikey & Me*. Brooke Warner, my publisher, Caitlyn Levin, my project manager, and everyone at She Writes Press for inspiration, patience, and for shepherding my book through the complex journey to publication. Jim Wooden, my cousin, for short notice help with JPEG, TIF, and DPI. John Wooden, my cousin, brother, and friend for shared memories, and for his unwavering support.

Resources I Discovered after I Completed Mikey & Me

Sibling Leadership Network (siblingleadership.org)
The purpose of the Sibling Leadership Network is to promote a broad network of siblings who share the experience of disability and people concerned with sibling issues by connecting them to social, emotional, governmental, and provisional supports across the lifespan enabling them to be effective advocates with their brother and sister, and to serve as change agents for themselves and their families.

The Sibling Support Project (siblingsupport.org)
The Sibling Support Project is the first national program dedicated to the life-long and ever-changing concerns of millions of brothers and sisters of people with special health, developmental, and mental health concerns.

What Siblings Would Like Parents and Service Providers to Know

I n the United States, there are over 4.5 million people who have special health, developmental, and mental health concerns. Most of these people have typically developing brothers and sisters. Brothers and sisters are too important to ignore, if for only these reasons:

- These brothers and sisters will be in the lives of family members with special needs longer than anyone. Brothers and sisters will be there after parents are gone and special education services are a distant memory. If they are provided with support and information, they can help their sibs live dignified lives from childhood to their senior years.

- Throughout their lives, brothers and sisters share many of the concerns that parents of children with special needs experience, including isolation, a need for information, guilt, concerns about the future, and caregiving demands. Brothers and sisters also face issues that are uniquely theirs including resentment, peer issues, embarrassment, and pressure to achieve.

Despite the important and life-long roles they will play in the lives of their siblings who have special needs, even the most family-friendly agencies often overlook brothers and sisters. Brothers and sisters, often left in the literal and figurative waiting rooms of service delivery systems, deserve better. True "family-centered" care and services will arrive when siblings are actively included in agencies' functional definition of "family."

The Sibling Support Project facilitated a discussion on Sib-Net, its online group for adult siblings of people with disabilities, regarding the considerations that siblings want from parents, other family members, and service providers. Below is a discussion of themes discussed by SibNet members and recommendations from the Sibling Support Project:

1. The Right to One's Own Life. Throughout their lives, brothers and sisters may play many different roles in the lives of their siblings who have special needs. Regardless of the contributions they may make, the basic right of siblings to their own lives must always be remembered. Parents and service providers should not make assumptions about responsibilities typically developing siblings may assume without a frank and open discussion. "Nothing about us without us"—a phrase popular with self-advocates who have disabilities—applies to siblings as well. Self-determination, after all, is for everyone—including brothers and sisters.

2. Acknowledging Siblings' Concerns. Like parents, brothers and sisters will experience a wide array of often-ambivalent emotions regarding the impact of their siblings' special needs. These feelings should be both expected and acknowledged by parents and other family members and service providers. Because most siblings will have the longest-lasting relationship with the family member who has a disability, these concerns will change over time. Parents and providers would be wise to learn more about siblings' life-long and ever-changing concerns.

3. Expectations for Typically Developing Siblings. Families need to set high expectations for all their children. However, some typically developing brothers and sisters react to their siblings' disability by setting unrealistically high expectations for themselves—and some feel they must somehow compensate for their siblings' special needs. Parents can help their typically developing children by conveying clear expectations and unconditional support.

4. Expect Typical Behavior From Typically Developing Siblings. Although difficult for parents to watch, teasing, name-calling, arguing and other forms of conflict are common among most brothers and sisters—even when one has special needs. While parents may be appalled at siblings' harshness toward one another, much of this conflict can be a beneficial part of normal social development. A child with Down syndrome who grows up with siblings with whom he sometimes fights will likely be better prepared to face life in the community as an adult than a child with Down syndrome who grows up as an only child. Regardless of how adaptive or developmentally appropriate it might be, typical sibling conflict is more likely to result in feelings of guilt when one sibling has special health or developmental needs. When conflict arises, the message sent to many brothers and sisters is, "Leave your sibling alone. You are bigger, you are stronger, you should know better. It is your job to compromise." Typically developing siblings deserve a life where they, like other children, sometimes misbehave, get angry, and fight with their siblings.

5. Expectations for the Family Member with Special Needs. When families have high expectations for their children who have special needs, everyone will benefit. As adults, typically-developing brothers and sisters will likely play important roles in the lives of their siblings who have disabilities. Parents can help siblings now by helping their children who have special needs acquire skills that will allow them to be as independent as possible as adults. To the extent possible, parents should have the same expectations for the child with special needs regarding chores and personal responsibility as they do for their typically developing children. Not only will similar expectations foster independence, it will also minimize the resentment expressed by siblings when there are two sets of rules—one for them, and another for their sibs who have special needs.

6. The Right to a Safe Environment. Some siblings live with brothers and sisters who have challenging behaviors. Other siblings assume responsibilities for themselves and their siblings that go beyond their age level and place all parties in vulnerable situations. Siblings deserve to have their own personal safety given as much importance as the family member who has special needs.

7. Opportunities to Meet Peers. For most parents, the thought of "going it alone," raising a child with special needs without the benefit of knowing another parent in a similar situation would be unthinkable. Yet, this routinely happens to brothers and sisters. Sibshops, online groups such as SibNet and SibTeen, and similar efforts offer siblings the common-sense support and validation that parents get from Parent-to-Parent programs and similar programs. Brothers and sisters—like parents—like to know that they are not alone with their unique joys and concerns.

8. Opportunities to Obtain Information. Throughout their lives, brothers and sisters have an ever-changing need for information about their sibling's disability, and its treatment and implications. Parents and service providers have an obligation to proactively provide siblings with helpful information. Any agency that represents a specific disability or illness and prepares materials for parents and other adults should prepare materials for siblings and young readers as well.

9. Sibs' Concerns about the Future. Early in life, many brothers and sisters worry about what obligations they will have toward their sibling in the days to come. Ways parents can reassure their typically-developing children are to make plans for the future of their children with special needs, involve and listen to their typically-developing children as they make these plans, consider backup plans, and know that siblings' attitude toward the extent of their involvement as adults may change over time. When brothers and sisters are "brought into the loop" and given the message early that they have their parents' blessing to pursue their dreams, their future involvement with their sibling will be a choice instead of an obligation. For their own good and for the good of their siblings who have disabilities, brothers and sisters should be afforded the right to their own lives. This includes having a say in whether and how they will be involved in the lives of their siblings who have disabilities as adults, and the level, type, and duration of involvement.

10. Including Both Sons and Daughters. Just as daughters are usually the family members who care for aging parents, adult sisters are usually the family members who look after the family member with special needs when parents no longer can. Serious exploration of sharing responsibilities among siblings—including brothers—should be considered.

11. Communication. While good communication between parents and children is always important, it is especially important in families where there is a child who has special needs. An evening course in active listening can help improve communication among all family members, and books, such as How to Talk So Kids Will Listen and Listen So Kids Will Talk and Siblings

Without Rivalry (both by Adele Faber and Elaine Mazlich) provide helpful tips on communicating with children.

12. One-on-One time with Parents. Children need to know from their parents' deeds and words that their parents care about them as individuals. When parents carve time out of a busy schedule to grab a bite at a local burger joint or window shop at the mall with their typically developing children, it conveys a message that parents "are there" for them as well and provides an excellent opportunity to talk about a wide range of topics.

13. Celebrate Every Child's Achievements and Milestones. Over the years, we've met siblings whose parents did not attend their high school graduation — even when their children were valedictorians—because the parents were unable to leave their child with special needs. We've also met siblings whose wedding plans were dictated by the needs of their sibling who had a disability. One child's special needs should not overshadow another's achievements and milestones. Families who seek respite resources, strive for flexibility, and seek creative solutions can help assure that the accomplishments of all family members are celebrated.

14. Parents' Perspective is More Important than the Actual Disability. Parents would be wise to remember that the parents' interpretation of their child's disability will be a greater influence on the adaptation of their typically developing sibling than the actual disability itself. When parents seek support, information, and respite for themselves, they model resilience and healthy attitudes and behaviors for their typically developing children.

15. Include Siblings in the Definition of "Family." Many educational, health care, and social service agencies profess a desire to offer family-centered services but continue to overlook the family members who will have the longest-lasting relationship with the person who has the special needs—the sisters and brothers.

When brothers and sisters receive the considerations and services they deserve, agencies can claim to offer "family-centered"— instead of "parent-centered"—services.

16. Actively Reach Out to Brothers and Sisters. Parents and agency personnel should consider inviting (but not requiring) brothers and sisters to attend informational, IEP, IFSP, and transition planning meetings, and clinic visits. Siblings frequently have legitimate questions that can be answered by service providers. Brothers and sisters also have informed opinions and perspectives and can make positive contributions to the child's team.

17. Learn More About Life as a Sibling. Anyone interested in families ought to be interested in siblings and their concerns. Parents and providers can learn more about "life as a sib" by facilitating a Sibshop, hosting a sibling panel, or reading books by and about brothers and sisters. Guidelines for conducting a sibling panel are available from the Sibling Support Project and in the Sibshop curriculum. Visit the Sibling Support Project's website for a bibliography of sibling-related books.

18. Create Local Programs Specifically for Brothers and Sisters. If your community has a Parent-to-Parent Program or similar parent support effort, a fair question to ask is: why isn't there a similar effort for the brothers and sisters? Like their parents, brothers and sisters benefit from talking with others who "get it." Sibshops and other programs for preschool, school age, teen, and adult siblings are growing in number. The Sibling Support Project, which maintains a database of over 450 Sibshops and other sibling programs, provides training and technical assistance on how to create local programs for siblings.

19. Include Brothers and Sisters on Advisory Boards and in Policies Regarding Families. Reserving board seats for siblings will give the board a unique, important perspective and reflect the agency's concern for the well being of brothers and sisters. Developing policies based on the important roles played by brothers and sisters will help assure that their concerns and contributions are a part of the agency's commitment to families.

20. Fund Services for Brothers and Sisters. No classmate in an inclusive classroom will have a greater impact on the social development of a child with a disability than brothers and sisters will. They will be their siblings' life-long "typically developing role models." As noted earlier, brothers and sisters will likely be in the lives of their siblings longer than anyone—longer than their parents and certainly longer than any service provider. For most brothers and sisters, their future and the future of their siblings with special needs are inexorably entwined. Despite this, there is little funding to support projects that will help brothers and sisters get the information, skills and support they will need throughout their lives. Governmental agencies would be wise to invest in the family members who will take a personal interest in the well being of people with disabilities and advocate for them when their parents no longer can. As one sister wrote: "We will become caregivers for our siblings when our parents no longer can. Anyone interested in the welfare of people with disabilities ought to be interested in us."

For more information contact:
Don Meyer
Sibling Support Project
A Kindering Center program
6512 23rd Ave NW #322
Seattle, WA 98117
206-297-6368
donmeyer@siblingsupport.org

about the author

Teresa Sullivan is a registered nurse with a master's degree in business administration. She has worked as a clinician, educator, and director of treatment programs specializing in addiction and mental health. She lives in Santa Monica, California with her adopted dogs, Danny, Maya, and Kate.

Author photo © Chris Loomis

Selected Titles from She Writes Press

She Writes Press is an independent publishing company founded to serve women writers everywhere. Visit us at www.shewritespress.com.

Make a Wish for Me: A Mother's Memoir by LeeAndra Chergey. $16.95, 978-1-63152-828-6. A life-changing diagnosis teaches a family that where's there is love there is hope—and that being "normal" is not nearly as important as providing your child with a life full of joy, love, and acceptance.

Godmother: An Unexpected Journey, Perfect Timing, and Small Miracles by Odile Atthalin. $16.95, 978-1-63152-172-0. After thirty years of traveling the world, Odile Atthalin—a French intellectual from a well-to-do family in Paris—ends up in Berkeley, CA, where synchronicities abound and ultimately give her everything she has been looking for, including the gift of becoming a godmother.

Rethinking Possible: A Memoir of Resilience by Rebecca Faye Smith Galli. $16.95, 978-1-63152-220-8. After her brother's devastatingly young death tears her world apart, Becky Galli embarks upon a quest to recreate the sense of family she's lost—and learns about healing and the transformational power of love over loss along the way.

Changed By Chance: My Journey of Triumph Over Tragedy by Elizabeth Barker. $16.95, 978-1-63152-810-1. When her dreams of parenthood and becoming a career mom take a nightmarish twist, Elizabeth Barker has to learn how to summon her inner warrior—for her and her family's survival.

Filling Her Shoes: Memoir of an Inherited Family by Betsy Graziani Fasbinder. $16.95, 978-1-63152-198-0. A "sweet-bitter" story of how, with tenderness as their guide, a family formed in the wake of loss and learned that joy and grief can be entwined cohabitants in our lives.

A Leg to Stand On: An Amputee's Walk into Motherhood by Colleen Haggerty. $16.95, 978-1-63152-923-8. Haggerty's candid story of how she overcame the pain of losing a leg at seventeen—and of terminating two pregnancies as a young woman—and went on to become a mother, despite her fears.